ᑭᐢᑭᓱᒥᑐᐠ KISKISOMITOK

ᑭᐢᑭᓱᒥᑐᐠ kiskisomitok

ᓀᐦᐄᔭᐤ to remind each and one another

ᑳᐯᓵᑳᐢᑌᐠ reuben quinn

editorial assistance by
Christine Stewart

foreword by
Savage Bear

Talonbooks

Talonbooks
9259 Shaughnessy Street, Vancouver, British Columbia, Canada V6P 6R4
talonbooks.com

Talonbooks is located on xʷməθkʷəy̓əm, Sḵwx̱wú7mesh, and səlilwətaɬ Lands.

Second printing: January 2026

Typeset in Gaduji, Minion 3 and Agenda One
Printed and bound in Canada on 100% post-consumer recycled paper

Cover illustration and design by Courteney Morin

Talonbooks acknowledges the financial support of the Canada Council for the Arts, the Government of Canada through the Canada Book Fund, and the Province of British Columbia through the British Columbia Arts Council and the Book Publishing Tax Credit.

Library and Archives Canada Cataloguing in Publication

Title: 880-01 kiskisomitok : nēhiyaw / kāpēsākāstēk = kiskisomitok : to remind each and one another
/ reuben quinn ; with editorial assistance by Christine Stewart.
Other titles: To remind each and one another
Names: Quinn, Reuben, author.
Description: Includes bibliographical references. | Includes text in English and nêhiyawêwin.
Identifiers: Canadiana 20240516230 | ISBN 9781772016444 (softcover)
Subjects: CSH: nêhiyawêwin—Study and teaching. | CSH: Cree language—Y dialect—Study and teaching. | CSH: Plains Cree language—Study and teaching. | CSH: nêhiyaw—Social life and customs. | CSH: Plains Cree—Social life and customs.
Classification: LCC PM989.Z9 P53 2025 | DDC 497/.3237—dc23

This book is dedicated to those who were told to forget their ways – after treaty was made and then broken. To the ones who were forbidden to remember and speak about their ways – in the residential schools and other institutions of colonization. They were jails, basically. To those ones who went underground within those institutions and continued to remember their ways through that time. To those who were resilient enough to remember their ways and carry those ways on. For those, I am forever grateful. For those who continue to speak our ways. For those, I am forever grateful. To those who continue to remind us of our ways, ᐑᓈᐦᑯᒫ *wînâhkomâ.*

what that is above it is powerful
what that is below it is powerful
the earth is my home

—Uncle Charles Gladue

Contents

Foreword

I am deeply humbled to write this foreword, and believe me when I tell you that you are in for a blessing; think of eating an oatmeal cookie with raisins, but the raisins turn out to be chocolate chips × 1,000. If you're holding this book and reading these words, take a moment to reflect on the countless events and connections that had to align across time and space to bring this book into your hands, right here, right now. Imagine the voices and teachings of countless ancestors, passed down through generations, now humbly offered to you within these pages. Many of reuben's teachings and experiences that have been passed down to him and through him can now resonate like an eternal echo. I hope these words stir something within you, as they have within me. reuben has opened his mind and heart to bring these words to you. He offers something for everyone, entwining universal themes of connection, love, and belonging, while inviting readers – whether they are ᓀᐦᐄᔭᐤ nêhîyaw or not – to learn, reflect, and grow through these teachings and stories. For those of us trying to make sense of a complex, fast-moving world of chaos and beauty, we can find a spiritual haven to rest and learn as we navigate the fragile threads of connection, resilience, and hope. The ᐊᑖᐦᑭᐯᔩᐦᑲᓇᐠ atâhkipêyîhkanak or spirit marker chart remains the foundation of reuben's teachings, and the design of this spiritual chart points in eight directions. In much the same way, this book gathers teachings from all directions, weaving them together with humility and love, as reuben gently honours his teachers by invoking their names throughout the text.

With a deep timbre inflected with joy, compassion, and humour, reuben's voice and presence captivate anyone within earshot, and as

I read his written words here in this book for the first time, I hear the gentle cadence of his voice in my mind. I've often jokingly called reuben the Cree-voice version of Morgan Freeman. Can voices embody the land? Listen to reuben and you just might believe this. I'm not sure when I first encountered reuben; perhaps it was in ceremony, or it may have been at the annual round dance at the University of Alberta, where he often taught classes. But it was when I was asked to serve as the Academic Lead for the creation of a massive open online course (MOOC) called Indigenous Canada and needed a voice to narrate parts of our video series that my thoughts turned to reuben. Offering tobacco, I approached him to share his voice and his thoughts when creating the MOOC. All of this he did incredibly well, but it wasn't just the MOOC work that stayed with me. I'd like to share one of his teachings, a profound reflection on the all-encompassing connection that unites the many nations across turtle island.

Prior to filming at the Faculty of Native Studies at the University of Alberta, reuben suggested we smudge before getting down to work – to start us off in a good way. I hadn't prearranged for this (as was policy at the U of A at the time), and thinking that we would trigger the smoke alarms and consequently the sprinklers, I said it would be too smoky to smudge. With a smile that danced quietly in the corner of his eyes but never touched his lips, reuben picked a single little leaf from my grape-sized sage bundle and said, "All we need is this." The comforting smoke of sage wafted up as he lit the small leaf between his thumb and finger ablaze. He said, "All you need to smudge is your good intent, that little bit of smoke is all you need." I said, "But what about the abalone shell, the matches, the eagle feather? Don't we need those to smudge?" He told me that the creator doesn't expect all those things from you, smudging is between you and the creator, it's not a performance, and there are no expectations or hard policies; kind intentions and prayer are all that is needed. "You do you," he said with a grin. I think about this moment a lot. This universal teaching is passed on through his father, who said, "ᐄᐧᔭᐚᐤᐁᑯᓯᐦᑲᐃᑑᑕᒪᐧᐠ wîyawâw êkosih ka itôtamwak," which means simply, "them, let them do it that way."

This teaching is also reflected in the Two Row Path (also known as Two Row Wampum Belt), called Teioháte Kaswenta in Kanien'kehá:ka Mohawk territory, made from the purple and white beads of quahog clam shells. Teioháte Kaswenta has a white background and two rows of purple beads running parallel across the sea of white. These parallel lines are canoes representing the Kanien'kehá:ka Mohawk Nation and the Nation of Denmark; the purple lines never intersect, nor do they collide or interfere with each other. They signal mutual respect and a bond between two hearts. This moment with reuben, as brief as it was, holds the simplicity and the complexity of Teioháte Kaswenta, too. That, nitôtêmtik, is the beauty of reuben's teachings; of many nêhîyawak and indigenous teachings. We can choose to make our own path in life, we are steering our own canoe, on our own journey. The teaching here is that we don't interfere with others' lives, belief systems, or value systems.

Although reuben is much too humble to say this, I often imagine his voice and the teachings that go with it like a softened smoke-tanned hide river carrying wisdom, warmth, and the weight of told and untold stories. Like smoke-tanned leather, reuben's words offer comfort, shelter, and warmth. Whether written or spoken, his nêhîyaw teachings and understandings that he shares come through clearly and powerfully. While many might call him elder, it is a title that reuben steadfastly refuses, and while he often uses the term kehteyahk for his own teachers, he does not take on that mantle, either. But he is a teacher, and what a teacher he is! For example, reuben teaches us that an unforced teardrop is the best offering. It is a blessing to have tears of gratitude, to be so full of happiness and joy that your body responds with an offering. Just reading the beauty of this concept is enough to bring you to tears. The wonderful thing about these teachings is that reuben peppers his script with humour all the way through. As I read his words about the unforced tear of gratitude, and as my tears began to build on the edge my eyes, he writes, "[tears are] good in ceremony but you can't script that stuff. Well, maybe some people can – pull a hair in your nostril!" So there I sat, reading about the unforced tear of gratitude, as my own tears spilled over between bursts of laughter. A good teacher can bring you tears, can bring you joy, love, and gratitude in the learnings. Our emotions are spaces to grow and learn, and I think extraordinary teachers understand these concepts completely.

So what better place for reuben to start than with this glorious word, sâkîyîtok – to love each and one another; after all, it is the first law of nêhîyawewak. I encourage you to embrace these concepts as you travel through this book. I want to remind you, as you embark on this reading journey, please linger, take this path slowly, savour the language and the teachings like the bite of a warm chocolate-chip cookie straight from your auntie's oven.

kitôtêm,
Savage
Citizen of Montreal Lake Cree Nation

How ᑭᐢᑭᓱᒥᑐᐠ kiskisomitok was composed

One day I was at the edge of my reserve. I looked out at the land beyond the reserve, and I realized that all that land beyond the reservation, all the colonized land beyond the reservation, this was the land of my ancestors, where their moccasins touched the earth. But colonization and genocide took our religion, our land, our faith, and our confidence. I wanted this book to bring back that reality that this was once the land that the moccasins of my ancestors touched, as far as the sun shone. I want the book to remind people that there was a way to live before colonization, and there still is, and it still works.

ᐯᑮᐍᐠ pêkîwek, all of you come home. That is what they say at the ᓂᐹᑵᓯᒨᐏᑲᒥᐠ nipâkwêsimôwikamik, the sundance – all of you come home, into the lodge, our big home.

In this book, there is no capitalization in ᓀᐦᐃᔭᐍᐏᐣ nêhîyawêwin. When you are sovereign and you don't owe anyone anything, then your name is in all lower case. It is my preference then that there are no capitals in ᓀᐦᐃᔭᐍᐏᐣ nêhîyawêwin in this book to show that it is a sovereign language. It's my style and I don't mean any disrespect. But this is the way this book is written.

Christine Stewart and I collaborated on this book. How did we do that? We taught together for five years in our Treaty Poetics class, and then we Zoomed and talked for several more years. In these meetings I was reminded of the teachings I had been given and what helped me. We recorded our meetings, and Christine transcribed the recording. Through this past year, we went over those conversations. In the summer, I went to the ᓂᐹᑵᓯᒨᐏᑲᒥᐠ

nipâkwêsimôwikamik, the sundance. I asked if I could write and I was told yes by ᑮᐦᑌᐊᔭᐦ kîhtêayah, the elder. I got permission and I decided what should be in the book.

ᐄᔩᓇᐊᐧᐠ ᐯᑮᐍᐧᐠ îyînawak pêkîwek

ᑳᐯᓵᑳᐢᑌᐠ

kâpêsâkâstek
reuben quinn

ᐊᒥᐢᑰᐊᐧᒌᐋᐧᐢᑲᐦᐄᐦᑲᓃᕽ ᐅᓅᒋᐦᑑᐃᐧᐲᓯᒼ
amiskôwacîwâskahîhkanîhk, onôcihtôwipîsim, 2025

ᐲᐦᑎᑵ ᑕᐚᐤ
pîhtikwê tawâw
come in, there is room!

I went to ceremony and made protocol and got my ᓀᐦᐄᔭᐤ nêhîyaw name. My name is ᑳᐯᓵᑳᐢᑌᐠ kâpêsâkâstek, the sun's rays just before you see the sun.

These are the teachings I have been given, as I understand them. And I am not a fluent speaker. As a ceremony person, teaching the ᓀᐦᐄᔭᐤ nêhîyaw spirit markers, as I was taught from the old ladies, I would like to pass them down to others in the same way. There are so many things that I cannot talk about because they are too sacred. I do my best with that. I smudge every morning upon awakening. I attend ᒫᑐᑎᓵᐣ mâtotisân, the sweat lodge ceremony, when I can. In the summer, when I can, I go to the ᓂᐹᑫᐧᓯᒨᐏᑲᒥᑲᐧᐦ nipâkwêsimôwikamikwah, the sundances. In working on this book, I am observing protocol, so this helps me. This chart that I share, I asked ᑮᐦᑌᐊᔭᐦ kîhtêayah, elder, Emma Gladue, out of Blue Quills, over there, if I could share it, and she said yes. So, I used to teach it in jails, but when I first presented it in Edmonton, I asked permission too for that. Can I do this? When I did my class presentation, in 2005, I asked ᑮᐦᑌᐊᔭᐦ kîhtêayah, elder, the late Jerome Wood to come in. I gave him tobacco to come and listen. Then I went to him after my presentation, and I said, "what do you think?" And he said to me, "ᒦᔫᐚᓯᐣ mîyôwâsin." So, I asked him, "can I share it in the community?" He said yes. I said okay. I think that laying down that foundation was what helped. Also, smudging with the students at the first class of the term and then at the last class. See, because that is what I have to do.

To preserve the spirit markers and the sounds, the syllables in the words that I know. To encourage others to do likewise, to preserve the beauty of our culture. It helps my mind a lot, looking at that eight-directional chart and learning the language from within. There are other systems. But this system works for me. It is ᒪᒫᐦᑖᐤ mamâhtâw! It is amazing! A paradigm shift happens in my mind! I want to encourage other ᓀᐦᐃᔭᐤ nêhîyaw learners with their minds, to think in a ᓀᐦᐃᔭᐤ nêhîyaw paradigm. I think it helps a lot.

ᑭᐢᓱᒥᑐᐠ kiskisomitok: to remind each and one another

The purpose of this book is to remind each other of where we are, to help prepare us for the day, for the moment, for the night. The purpose of this book is to introduce us to the spirit markers, to remind us of the first four laws, to help us to think, and to keep reminding each other, to keep talking to each other, helping each other understand. For us two-legged people, to help us connect with each other to build and have relationships with each other and with the other five nations – the winged people, the four-legged people, the plant people, the insect people, and the water people.

I ask myself, what can we leave them with? The reader. What can we give them that they can take away with them? I want this to be a gentle book. What is this book for? I would like this book to help people. It made me feel better when I started, when I started relearning the language and the spirit markers. It helped me with my self-worth. It made me feel whole and helped me feel part of a community of language speakers and learners. It helped me understand ceremony. Going back to the language and culture just helped me let go of some of that shame and to begin to learn how to forgive. I am ᐚᐦᔭᐑᐢ wâhyawîs. I have a ways to go yet.

When you forgive, ᐸᑭᑌᔩᐦᑕᐦ pakitêyîhtah, you actually live.

ᐸᑭᑌᔩᐦᑕᒫᐑᐣ pakitêyîhtamâwîn is to let something go with your mind.

I want to focus on positive words, awakening the positive, awakening the positive words, the concepts that hold life.

One of the words I would like to use in this book is ᐄᐄᐧᒉᐢᑰᐊᐧᑭᓂᑯᔭᐦ îwîcêskôwakinikoyah, someone is moulding us, and it is the creator moulding us.

When the old people talk, I hear that word and that it is to remind us to respect the elements and the plants, that ᒪᓂᑑᐤ manitôw, creator, is moulding us from all of these elements. A really old word that one, ᐄᐄᐧᒉᐢᑰᐊᐧᑭᓂᑯᔭᐦ îwîcêskôwakinikoyah, I have been taught that the word is very important because it refers to the moulding of the human being, that we were all moulded in that way by ᒪᓂᑑᐤ manitôw. I have been taught by those who live and speak the ways of the old people that this word expresses who we are and where we come from – the elements. That we come from the elements and that word reminds us of that. I have heard this word many times in ceremonial or community gatherings – ᐄᐄᐧᒉᐢᑰᐊᐧᑭᓂᑯᔭᕽ îwîcêskôwakinikoyahk.

I was told that ᐋᔩ âyî is the name we have for the supreme deity, the supreme being, in ᓀᐦᐄᔭᐤ nêhîyaw language. It is such a holy reference, it is mostly used in ceremony. Now only the first part ᐋ â is used in ceremony and rarely will you hear the whole name. It is such a holy word that I will not be using the whole name from here on in. Instead, I will use ᐋ â.

We are conceived in the heart of ᐋ â.

We owe each other everything – all six nations.

It is the connection that is sacred. It is our connections that are sacred. Touch the earth. Reorient yourself. Remember your ancestors and their footsteps.

My dad said, “ᑭᐢᑭᓯᐦ ᐃᑌᐦ ᐄᑮ ᐱᒧᐦᑌᒋᐠ ᑭᒨᓰᒪᐠ ᐁᑿᐦ ᑯᐦᑯᒪᐠ kiskisih itêh îkî pimotêcik kimosômak êkwah kohkomak.” Remember where they walked, your grandfathers and your grandmothers.

“ᐁᑿᐦ ᐃᑌᐦ ᐄᑮ ᐃᑕᐦᑯᐢᑳᑖᐦᑭᐠ ᐊᐢᑮᐦ ᐅᒪᐢᑭᓯᓅᐚᐘᐦ êkwah itêh îkî itahkoskâtâhkik askîh omaskisinôwâwah.” Where their moccasins touched the earth.”

As I touch the earth, I remember that, that they touched that earth.

My grandmother, my dad’s mother, walked the earth where I grew up. Her English name was Marie Batoche and she and her four other sisters came from ᒥᐢᑕᐦᐃᒪᐢᑿᐦ mistahi-maskwah, big bear’s people.[1] I heard there was five sisters. She picked medicines from the sloughs, the hills, and the prairies from where I grew up. Her ᒪᐢᑭᓯᓇᐦ maskisinah touched that earth.

ᑭᐢᑭᓱᒥᑐᐠ kiskisomitok – to remind each and one another.

Our strands of dna take us back to that 14.8 billion years ago – to the beginning of this universe.[2] We already know what we need to know within our dna because we were conceived at that point of origin. ᓰᓰᑿᐣ sîsîkwan, the rattle, reminds of us that. ᓰᓰᑿᐣ sîsîkwan was the first sound. It is the first sound. We exist in the heart of ᐋ, in both times, then and now, and all times.

We just need to remind each other. To talk to each other.

---

1 The reason I am using lower case for big bear’s name is that he specifically voiced his sovereignty.

2 I just heard that someone is suggesting now that it is closer to twenty-six billion years.

ᑭᐢᑭᓱᒥᑐᐠ kiskisomitok – remind each and one another
ᑭᐢᑭᓯᐦ kiskisih – you remember
ᑲᑭᐢᑭᓱᒥᑎᐣ kakiskisomitin – I will remind you
ᑭᐢᑭᓱᒼ kiskisom – remind him or her or it

The chart is ᑭᐢᑯᓅᐚᒌᐦᒋᑲᐣ kiskonôwâcîhcikan, a legend, a map, or a medicine wheel (this is the term most commonly used these days). Literally, ᑭᐢᑯᓅᐚᒌᐦᒋᑲᐣ kiskonôwâcîhcikan means, "you look at it, you memorize it to learn what the next step is to be."

There are circular patterns of stone across the prairies, giving the people directions. They are now known as a medicine wheel. These ᑭᐢᑯᓅᐚᒌᐦᒋᑲᓇᐠ kiskonôwâcîhcikanak are sacred and were used as maps. They were designed to help people live.

One ᑭᐢᑯᓅᐚᒌᐦᒋᑲᐣ kiskonôwâcîhcikan is the chart of ᐊᑖᐦᑭᐯᔩᐦᑲᓇᐠ atâhkipêyîhkanak, the spirit markers. It helps people's lives by embodying a ᓀᐦᐄᔭᐤ nêhîyaw paradigm, a ᓀᐦᐄᔭᐤ nêhîyaw world view.

So, the word ᑭᐢᑯᓅᐚᒌᐦᒋᑲᐣ kiskonôwâcîhcikan describes the instrument in front of you (see pages 24 and 25). In this case, that instrument is the chart. It is a ᑭᐢᑯᓅᐚᒌᐦᒋᑲᐣ kiskonôwâcîhcikan, a legend, map,
or medicine wheel.

And what can I say about ᑭᐢᑯᓅᐚᒌᐦᒋᐦᑲᓇᐠ kiskônawâcîhcihkanak? They are there to guide us to a destination and the chart also shows us a destination. That destination is a paradigm shift, a shift in consciousness and perception.

As I understand it, everyone has an obligation, and so those spirit markers also have obligations, and those obligations are to bring us the laws and principles they hold within, to remind us,

ᑲᑭᐢᑭᓱᒥᑹᔮᐦᑭᐠ kakiskisomikwêyâhkik. They are here to guide and remind us.

So, this book is based in the spirit markers and the first four laws in the spirit markers.

We have ᐋᐦᑭᐯᔩᐦᑲᓇᐠ atâhkipêyîhkanak, the large spirit markers, and ᐋᒑᐦᑭᐯᔩᐦᑲᓂᓴᐠ acâhkipêyîhkanisak, the little ones – the small spirit markers on the side. The ᐊᑖᐦᑭᐯᔩᐦᑲᓇᐠ atâhkipêyîhkanak are our writing system – each large spirit marker represents a sound, holds a law and the spirit of that law. I don't know much about the small spirit markers, but they are the ones that link everything when something needs to be linked.

And this is what I teach and how I teach ᓀᐦ᐀ᔭᐍᐏᐣ nêhîyawêwin: with the spirit markers.

Everyone gets something different. Students always say this, that they had a moment of "aha," and me too. This happens.

And I teach the way the old ladies talked to me, enunciating every syllable of a word.

ᐊ ᓵᑮᔩᑐᐠ **a** sâkîyîtok[3] – love each and one another
ᐸ ᐑᒌᔩᑐᐠ **pa** wîcîyîtok – help each and one another
ᑕ ᒦᔪᐚᑕᒧᐠ **ta** mîyowâtamok – be happy, have fun, enjoy
ᓚ ᓲᐦᑲᐢᑤᐠ **la** sôhkastwâk – be disciplined, make it strong, stay strong

Why only four laws? Because that is enough. That is lots. Some of the other laws are referenced in the glossary and throughout the book and all the laws are woven into each other. But, as my

3 You will also see this as ᓵᑭᐦᐃᑐᐠ sâkihitok.

brother Carl always says, if you get the first law, ᐊ ᓵᑮᔩᑐᐠ sâkîyîtok, love each and one another, then the others are woven into place. It is the first law that weaves, ᐄᐦ ᐊᔭᐲᐦᑳᑖᐦ îh ayapîhkâtâh, all of the forty-three other laws into place.

And these ᓀᐦᐃᔭᐤ nêhîyaw laws are telling us to do something.

ᐳᑯᐦ ᑲᑭᐢᑭᓰᔭᕽ ᐆᒪᐦ pokoh kakiskisîyahk[4] ômah – we have to remember this, where we are

The earth holds us.

We are spinning and yet we do not fall off.

We need to remember.

We need to tell each other stories, the old stories.

ᑭᐢᑭᓯᒥᑐᐠ kiskisomitok.

We need to remind each and one another of natural law: that the sun rises in the east and sets in the west, that ᑮᓯᑳᐤ kîsikâw, the day, is the illumination of the sacred spirit. That ᑮᓯᐠ kîsik is a sacred spirit. The sun, ᐲᓯᒼ pîsim, is an ᐅᑮᓯᑰ okîsikôw. It is a spirit. It rises and sets upon this land and the sun says, "everything I touch, I am related to." This was taught to me by Kanien'kehá:ka Mohawk ᑮᐦᑌᐊᔭᐦ kîhtêayah, elder, John Cree. And that animates the sun, right. So, I started thinking about symbiosis, and remembering symbiosis as sacred and photosynthesis as love.

4 This means blood memory.

The trees, they reach out and they reach up and that is how we are taught to pray, in their manner. And that is called ᓲᓂᐢᑫ sôniskê, that is called reaching out and up.

That is their ᑳᑮᔩᓯᒨᐏᐣ kâkîyisimôwin. This is their prayer and their prayer is answered in the process of photosynthesis and through their gratitude that oxygen is produced.

And so, we also remind each other of the importance of ᔫᑎᐣ yôtin, the wind. ᔫᑎᐣ yôtin, so important, it brings us that oxygen from the plants and the trees. ᔫᑎᐣ yôtin is everywhere.

ᑖᔨᐢᑯᐨ ᑭᒧᓲᒥᓇᐤ ᔫᑎᐣ ᑲ ᑭᐢᑭᓱᒫᔭᐦ
tâyiskoc kimosôminaw yôtin ka kiskisomâyah
For instance, our grandfather wind, to remember him.
ᔫᑎᐣ yôtin our grandfather, the wind, for us to remember him.
And to remind each other of ᓵᑭᐸᑳᐤ sâkipakâw, earth love. The earth loves us more than we can know.

To remind each other of the prophesies ᑭᐢᑰᐍᔩᐦᑫᐏᓇᐦ kiskôwêyîhkewinah, the great cleansings that are coming. There we are reminded, ᐘᐍᔩᐠ waweyîk, prepare yourselves, for all of those: the wind, the water, the earth, the fire. Hold your pipes close, your bundles, and what they mean by that is, "hold your faith close to you." That is how we prepare ourselves – by being spiritually alive. By remembering the things we need to do: picking sweetgrass, giving it away, etc., etc.

ᒪᐢᑯᓰᔫᐑᐦᑲᐢᐠ maskosîyôwîhkask – the hay's sweetgrass
ᒥᐢᑕᑎᒨᐑᐦᑲᐢᐠ mistatimôwîhkask – the horse's sweetgrass (sage)
ᒧᐢᑐᐢᐆᐑᐦᑲᐢᐠ mostosôwîhkask – the buffalo's sweetgrass (sundance sage)
ᐊᒥᐢᑰᐑᐦᑲᐢᐠ amiskôwîhkask – the beaver's sweetgrass (wild mint)

When you are on the land you start remembering – the land helps you remember.

To remind each other of love.

To remind each other of natural law.

To remind each other that we are conceived in the heart of ᐋ, the supreme being.

Like ᐊᑖᐦᑭᐯᔩᐦᑲᓇᐠ atâhkipêyîhkanak, the spirit markers, those mnemonic devices, this book is meant to help us think, to remind each other.

ᐲᑭᐢᑳᑎᑐᐠ pîkiskwâtitok, to talk to each other, and to remind each other of natural law. All of this information for a good life is held within the spirit markers and the chart. And maybe we should just put the word ᑭᑐᐦ kitoh in there. It is shorter than ᐲᑭᐢᑳᑎᑐᐠ pîkiskwâtitok, ᑭᑐᐦ kitoh.

ᑭᑐᐦ kitoh means "talking." It is kind of like us using our communication device. When the elk are communicating with each other, we call that ᑭᑐᐦ kitoh. When crows are using their voices, we call that ᑭᑐᐦ kitoh. If you were to say that to everyone, to use their voices, it would be ᑭᑐᐠ kitok.

Oh my, I was just thinking about that this morning. Like how they, ᓀᐦᐃᔭᐘᐠ the nêhîyawak, used to communicate before. Like from where we went. Where you took me to, that place, that nice place – rib stone. That's where they, ᓀᐦᐃᔭᐘᐠ the nêhîyawak, would have had their smoke signals. There on a hill. But I wonder how else they communicated? There had to be a line of communication somehow. I guess runners and the criers.

reuben quinn: I was eleven years old when I encountered the spirit markers, when Mrs. Houle brought the teachings in.

Christine Stewart: Do you actually remember that class?

rq: Yes.

CS: That moment?

rq: Yes. I do. I remember Mrs. Houle's big glasses. They were, what do you call those glasses? Indian Affairs glasses. But she is so kind to me, anyways. Because I'm, I'm her godson. Yeah, well, I had just gotten my hearing back, as well, because I'd been deaf for so long. Had difficulties hearing. So, when I did get my hearing back, it was, it was with those old ladies. That were talking to me and I could hear them enunciate. And I remember before I lost my hearing. Before residential day school, I remember that all I spoke was ᓀᐦᐃᔭᐍᐏᐣ nêhîyawêwin. Yeah, that's all I understood. And then when those old ladies came, they were talking the same way I heard, so I knew how to articulate right away, how to put my tongue and my lips in place, my tongue and my lips to sound like a native speaker. So, I was very lucky that way, I guess. Misfortune brings good fortune. I was sent to the Charles Camsell Indian Hospital where they did experimental surgery on me. It worked. I guess. I lost my hearing for a time. When I got it back, it was blessed with ᓀᐦᐃᔭᐍᐏᐣ nêhîyawêwin. I was blessed with ᓀᐦᐃᔭᐍᐏᐣ nêhîyawêwin.

CS: How did you lose your hearing?

rq: Ear infections damaged the anvil and the eardrum. I remember my mom would always be speaking to me and she spoke to me in ᓀᐦᐃᔭᐤ nêhîyaw.

CS: Did she go to residential school?

rq: She went to residential school.

The ᐄᔩᓈᐤ îyînaw[5] writing systems have always been in nature. We have always had our own writing systems. There is that one spirit marker found at Writing-on-Stone, ᐊ, it verifies that.[6]

The ᓀᐦᐄᔭᐤ nêhîyaw ᐊᑖᐦᑭᐯᔩᐦᑲᓇᐠ atâhkipêyîhkanak, spirit markers, are all the animals' tracks and the sounds they make.

And like I said, ᐊᑖᐦᑭᐯᔩᐦᑲᓇᐠ atâhkipêyîhkanak, our spirit markers, are large and small: ᐊᑖᕽ atâhk, large spirit, and ᐊᒑᕽ acâhk, small spirit.

The words "large" and "small" don't do them justice.

ᐊ, the first one, a, the first spirit marker, was found at Writing-on-Stone and it is reputed to be ten thousand years old. I was told this by the archaeologist who worked with the late Dr. Anne Anderson.

One story is that i t was ᒥᐢᑕᓇᐢᑯᕀᐍᐤ mistanaskowêw, Badger Being or Calling Badger, who had a vision of the spirit markers. It came to him from the creator passed down to the ones that sit with the creator, those ones. I don't want to mention them right now. In the vision, he was given direction to pass ᐊᑖᐦᑭᐯᔩᐦᑲᓇᐠ atâhkipêyîhkanak, the spirit markers, on. He was instructed to show them to another person, ᒫᒌᔨᒥᓈᐦᑎᐠ mâcîyiminâhtik,

5 îyinaw and îyînaw are both correct. Today you will mostly hear îyinaw. But I love this one, îyînaw, the best. Because it is how the old people would say it.

6 Writing-on-Stone / Áísínai'pi, parks.canada.ca/culture/spm-whs/sites-canada/sec02t.

who then taught them to the people. The ᒥᐢᑕᓇᐢᑲᐍᐤ mistanaskowêw narrative is a spirit marker origin story. This comes to me from Carl Quinn and Jerry Saddleback.

According to European history, James Evans, a Methodist minister, invented the syllabic writing system, and he came up with the writing system within six months. But they were not invented by James Evans. There is a lot of research on this that you can read.[7]

I learned ᐊᑖᐦᑭᐯᔩᐦᑲᓇᐠ atâhkipêyîhkanak, the spirit markers, at eleven, turning twelve years old. After the Blue Quills Residential School system was shut down in 1970, the Blue Quills Native Education Council (Cold Lake, Kehewin, Heart Lake, Beaver Lake, Saddle Lake/Whitefish Lake/Good Fish Lake,[8] Frog Lake) took over the building,[9] and I studied with the late Rosanna Houle. That was in 1971. We were coming out of genocide and some time before that year, in order to bring the teachings into the school, Caroline Hunter and Rosanna Houle, and I don't know who else, went to see ᐱᐦᐁᐤ pihêw, the old man. And they learned from ᐱᐦᐁᐤ pihêw. He was a highly regarded and revered ᑮᐦᑌᐊᔭᐦ kîhtêayah, elder, from Goodfish Lake, Alberta. He taught them about the spirit markers, and he said, "ᒪᓂᑑᐤ ᐄ ᑮ ᒦᔩᑯᔭᐦ manitôw î kî mîyîkoyah, creator, gave them to us." Then Rosanna Houle taught us. She would spend time with me, and then I remembered them again when I was

---

7 See "Good resources that you might like to follow up with" at the back of this book.

8 Saddle Lake, Good Fish Lake, and Whitefish Lake used to be all one reservation.

9 This was achieved after a seventeen-day sit-in started by Stanley Redcrow and other parents; see "How Stanley Redcrow and First Nations activists reclaimed the Blue Quills Residential School," *cbc.ca*, May 10, 2017. The school is now an accredited university – University nuhelot'ine thaiyots'i nistameyimâkanak Blue Quills.

older. So, I am a ᓀᐦᐄᔭᐍᐏᐣ nêhîyawêwin teacher – for the past twenty years, and I have always taught ᓀᐦᐄᔭᐍᐏᐣ nêhîyawêwin with the ᐊᑖᐦᑭᐯᔩᐦᑲᓇᐠ atâhkipêyîhkanak, spirit markers, because that is how I was taught, to preserve a more precise pronunciation of ᓀᐦᐄᔭᐍᐏᐣ nêhîyawêwin, to preserve the number of syllables, to preserve each syllable and the law they hold, to preserve the words that were used in the original way, according to our generation. Through the generations we have lost many words, and with them laws, culture, and traditions. Now we have to remember and to remind each other of those words.

The spirit markers are so vital in learning ᓀᐦᐄᔭᐍᐏᐣ nêhîyawêwin because they mark the exact sounds of ᓀᐦᐄᔭᐍᐏᐣ nêhîyawêwin. ᓀᐦᐄᔭᐤ nêhîyaw law is embedded in ᓀᐦᐄᔭᐍᐏᐣ nêhîyawêwin; language revitalization lives in the stories within the language. The language moves in ideas, and so the correct articulation of the sounds of ᓀᐦᐄᔭᐍᐏᐣ nêhîyawêwin, of the spirit markers, is important.

At Blue Quills, they did research on language and one of the findings by Carl Quinn, who worked there at the time, was that we were losing a syllable in ᓀᐦᐄᔭᐍᐏᐣ nêhîyawêwin per generation through contractions. The aspiration, ᐦ, the small spirit marker *h*, is also often dropped. Standard Roman orthography, otherwise known as SRO, readily marks the elisions. It eliminates a syllable and therefore we lose a spirit marker with each contraction. Eliminate, that is a good word. Using SRO eliminates ᐊᑖᐦᑭᐯᔩᐦᑲᓇᐠ atâhkipêyîhkanak, the spirit markers. Since each ᐊᑖᐦᑭᐯᔩᐦᑲᐣ atâhkipêyîhkan, spirit marker, holds a law, each is a sovereign being; each loss of a syllable is a loss of the understanding of that being or law.

Like the greeting ᑖᓂᓯ ᑮᔭᐦ tânisi kîyah, it had been shortened to ᑖᓂᓯᐦ tânisih. Then it went to ᑖᐣᓯ tânsi and, in some cases, to ᑕᐣᐢ tâns.

From ᑖᓂᓯ ᑮᔭᐦ to ᑕᐣᐢ, that's a lot of missing ᐊᑖᐦᑭᐯᔩᐦᑲᓇᐠ atâhkipêyîḥkanak, spirit markers, and their laws.

Noah Cardinal, one of the most gifted language speakers in Saddle Lake, grew up in the 1930s and 1940s and he said, "if I went back one hundred years, I wouldn't understand the grandfathers," because the language has changed so much. I have heard people call it linguicide. These languages were sleeping and ᐄᔩᓇᐤ îyînaw have been waking them up.

How many ᓀᐦᐃᔭᐍᐏᐣ nêhîyawêwin words there are now in the language? Yeah, 30,000 words the last time I heard. It's quite a bit, quite a big drop from 600,000 words. And you know, those 600,000 words just weren't in one area, because we, the ᓀᐦᐃᔭᐤ nêhîyaw people, go all the way from the Rocky Mountains, over to the eastern side of turtle island, all along the Eastern Seaboard into Florida. My relative there, Jerry Saddleback, he says that when he went down to South America, they had the same word for fire as we do here. So they had those 600,000 words, and whatever they knew, they had to keep those and keep passing them on – those ᓀᐦᐃᔭᐤ nêhîyaw societies.

ᑭᐢᑭᓱᒥᑐᐠ kiskisomitok, to remind each other – and how you will hear it nowadays is ᑭᐢᑭᓱᐨᑐᐠ kiskisom'tok. Yeah, we have so many shortcuts nowadays in ᓀᐦᐃᔭᐍᐏᐣ nêhîyawêwin. And I believe very strongly, wholeheartedly, that the reason why we are in this situation is because of colonial policy. Those ᐅᑮᐦᒌᐦᑖᐤ ᐃᐢᑫᐘᐠ okîhcîhtwâw iskwêwak, highly revered, highly respected females with jurisdiction over languages and medicines – they were not honoured or recognized by the colonial government.

The colonial government would only deal with the chief and council system that they had created for registered "Indians." ᐅᑮᐦᒌᐦᑣᐤ ᐃᐢᑵᐘᐠ the okîhcîhtwâw iskwêwak have to be honoured. They had two departments – the department of medicine and pharmacology and the department of languages. There were 600,000 words and whatever words they knew, they had to keep passing them on. And who were the first ones that were attacked during colonization? Those females, eh.

I say "females" – not "women." Because woman, as I understand it, means "wife of man." I say "females" because they were not property. I don't know how to explain it. They are sovereign. Such a different system.

And so, with each syllable loss is the loss of ᐊᑖᐦᑭᐯᔩᐦᑲᐣ atâhkipêyîhkan, a spirit marker. And each ᐊᑖᐦᑭᐯᔩᐦᑲᐣ atâhkipêyîhkan holds the meaning of life within its own context. I think that's why those old ladies, when they'd talk to me, they'd enunciate every syllable of the word. And I do remember one old lady always saying to me, "ᑖᓂᓯ ᓅᓯᓯᒼ tânisi nosisim." And I didn't understand ᑖᓂᓯ tânisi, with its extra syllable, because all the kids around me said ᑖᐣᓯ tânsi. I didn't understand that it was the same word. I think it is confusing for people who want to learn when they encounter the long version of the words, the number of syllables.

Like I said, learning ᓀᐦᐄᔭᐍᐏᐣ nêhîyawêwin through the spirit markers teaches the student the correct articulation. They are phonetically on target. This is not true of SRO, standard Roman orthography. Although it is very helpful, there are sounds that are not represented in SRO. It cannot represent the original sounds.

ᓀᐦᐄᔭᐍᐏᐣ nêhîyawêwin contains the primal sounds of the human as made by human babies. When I'm teaching about sounds in class, I always reference babies while they still have their, what is it called? The fontanelle, that soft spot. While the fontanelle is really soft and hasn't started closing yet, the only sounds the children can make are crying sounds or giggling sounds, and then the next sound they start to make is cooing sounds. But you listen to a child coo, they'll go ᑯ ᑯ ᑯ ᑯ koo koo koo. And you listen to a ᐊ. And then the next sound they make is usually ᐸᐸᐸᐸ pa pa pa pa. You'll hear babies saying that as the fontanelle starts closing. And then as they begin to develop their own language and communication, these little babies, they start incorporating the other consonant sounds that we'll hear. Usually ᑲᑲᑲᑲ ka ka ka ka. And if you listen to a baby make those consonant sounds, those are the sounds of ᓀᐦᐄᔭᐁᐧᐃᐧᐣ nêhîyawêwin.

When we articulate the sounds of ᓀᐦᐄᔭᐁᐧᐃᐧᐣ nêhîyawêwin as they are represented in the spirit markers, we express the rhythms and sounds of the land the language comes from. ᓀᐦᐄᔭᐁᐧᐃᐧᐣ nĉhîyawêwin comes from the land.

Every time the old people talked about our language, they said,

"ᒪᓂᑑᐤᐄᑮ ᒦᔩᑯᔭᐦ manitôwîkî mîyîkoyah."

That is what the old people always said, "the creator gave it to us," the ᓀᐦᐄᔭᐤ nêhîyaw language.

ᓀᐦᐄᔭᐁᐧᐃᐧᐣ nêhîyawêwin is an expression, a manifestation of the land. It holds the prints of the animals, the sounds of the animals. It holds the early sounds of the human being. It holds sounds and sensations of the elements, ᐃᐢᑯᑌᐤ iskotêw, the fire, ᐊᐢᑮᐩ askîy, the earth, ᓂᐲᐩ nipîy, the water, and ᔫᑎᐣ yôtin, the wind.

ᐄᐱᐦᑎᑫᐧᔮᒧᐦᑫᐧᔮᐦᑭᐠ îpihtikweyâmohkweyâhkik.

What this means is that we get infused with those elements. And so, from there the birds are given their ᑭᑐᐦ kitoh, their speech, and the beavers are given their ᑭᑐᐦ kitoh, their speech. And the rest of the four nations, including us two-legged people. We all have our own ᑭᑐᐦ kitoh, our own ways to speak.

And so, the spirit markers were given us by the creator. I was told that this was a complicated process, the passing down of the spirit markers. But I am unable to talk about it here. ᐊᑖᐦᑭᐯᔩᐦᑲᓇᐠ atâhkipêyîhkanak, spirit markers, express the beauty of those elements, of those beings. Those ᐊᑖᐦᑭᐯᔩᐦᑲᓇᐠ atâhkipêyîhkanak remind us of those beings, of that beauty, of that love. They are a map, a legend, that marks a path. It reminds us of how to be, to be together, to be spiritually alive.

Through them we learn how to honour, uphold, celebrate the laws, ᓵᑮᔩᑐᐃᐧᐣ sâkîyitowin, ᐄᐧᒌᔩᑐᐃᐧᐣ wîcîyitowin, ᒦᔪᐋᐧᑕᒨᐃᐧᐢ mîyowâtamôwin, ᐁᑲᐧᐦ êkwah, ᓲᐦᑲᐢᑖᐧᐃᐧᐣ sôhkastwâwin, and the other forty spirit marker laws.

It is elemental and in this elemental way ᓀᐦᐄᔭᐁᐧᐃᐧᐣ nêhîyawêwin is infused with treaty sensibility, treaty 6[10] and the foundations of our laws.

Each spirit marker lies in a cardinal direction, a grandfather or grandmother direction, and holds a law that embodies a way

10 For the indigenous nations who negotiated the numbered treaties with the Crown, all of those treaties were sacred and sovereign entities. That is why I am not using capital letters when I mention treaty 6. Because it is a sacred and sovereign entity. The colonial powers did not see the numbered treaties in this way. To the colonial powers, those treaties were only transactional. Further, the Crown did not even honour the treaties in their own terms – as transactional agreements. A colonial understanding of treaty 6 would use capitals. But I do not have this understanding. I honour treaty 6 as it is – sacred and sovereign.

to live on this earth in healthy relations, as a respectful and supportive relative. Each spirit marker is a law, and each law embodies a form of ᒥᔫᐚᐦᑯᐦᑑᐃᐧᐣ mîyôwâhkohtôwin, the spirit of good relations. By learning ᓀᐦᐃᔭᕀᐁᐧᐃᐧᐣ nêhîyawêwin through the spirit markers, we learn about the connection of all people to the land – insect people, winged people, four-legged people, plant people, water people, and two-legged (human) people. And we learn the ways in which we need to honour those laws and relations. Learning ᓀᐦᐃᔭᕀᐁᐧᐃᐧᐣ nêhîyawêwin through ᐊᑖᐦᑭᐯᔩᐦᑲᓇᐠ atâhkipêyîhkanak, the spirit markers, reminds us of our relationship with the earth and treaty follows those laws.

Now, every spirit marker has a purpose.

For instance, **ᑲ** ka is something that "will be." **ᐯ** pe means "come this way," ᐯᑐᐦᑌ petohteh means "come hither" or "come here." ᐯᒦᒋᓱᐦ pemîciso means "come eat." And so that one **ᐱ** pi, it has a function too, and then ᐱᒼ pim has it also.

In this case, ᐱᒼ pim, its function is to find words that are filled with the meaning of life, as it is from its perspective, that spirit marker's perspective – ᐱᒫᑎᓲᐃᐧᐣ pimâtisôwin, life. Everything that has ᐱᒼ pim in it is about life – **ᐱ** pi, ᐱᒼ pim.

The form of the spirit markers holds their meaning and significance. Like, the centre of the chart always remains empty. It is ᐸᐦᑕᒫ pahtamâ, the place of origin, beyond heaven, ᐸᐦᑕᒫ pahtamâ. It also represents the hole where the ᓀᐦᐃᔭᐊᐧᐠ nêhîyawak came to earth as stardust. This is also represented in the patch of bare earth in the ᓂᐹᑫᐧᓯᒨᐃᐧᑲᒥᐠ nipâkwêsimôwikamik, the sundance.

ᐊᑖᐦᑭᐯᔩᐦᑲᓇᐠ
atâhkipêyîhkanak
the spirit markers

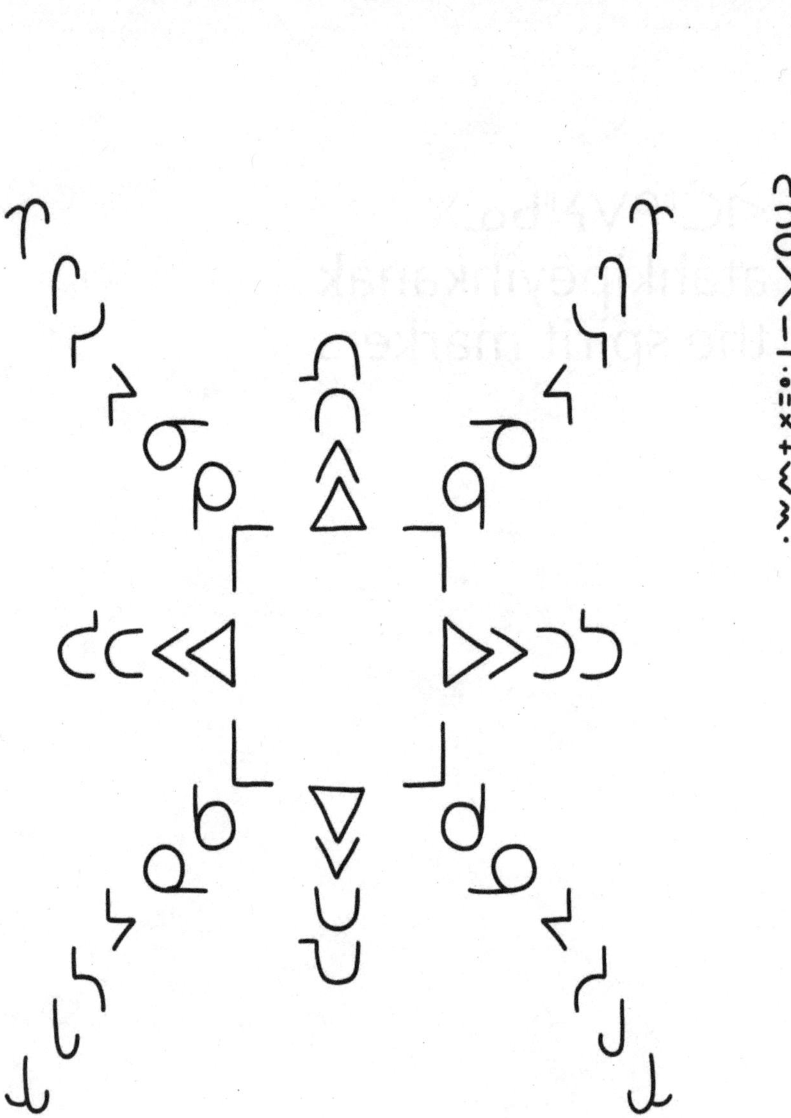

ᐊᑖᐦᑭᐯᔩᐦᑲᓇᐠ atâhkipêyîhkanak
the spirit markers
drawn by Courteney Morin

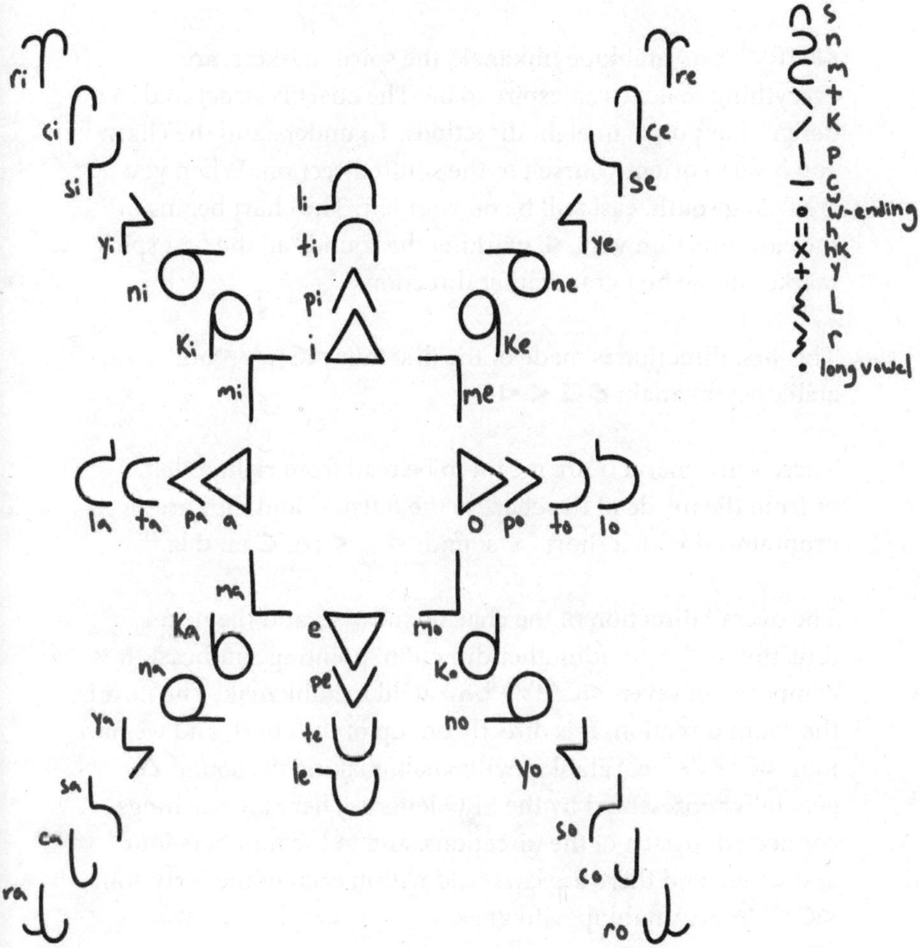

ᐊᑖᐦᑭᐯᔩᐦᑲᓇᐠ atâhkipêyîhkanak
the spirit markers marked with standard Roman orthography (SRO)
drawn by Courteney Morin

ᐊᑖᐦᑭᐯᔩᐦᑲᓇᐠ atâhkipêyîhkanak, the spirit markers, are everything that we can aspire to be. The chart is structured in a design that points in eight directions. To understand the chart, you have to orient yourself to the south direction. When you are facing south, east will be on your left. The chart begins in the east direction with **ᐊ**, marking the sound "a," the first spirit marker in the first grandfather direction.

This first direction is made of the first four ᐊᑖᐦᑭᐯᔩᐦᑲᓇᐠ atâhkipêyîhkanak: **ᓚ ᑕ ᐸ ᐊ**.

These spirit markers are meant to be read from right to left, or from the inside of the chart to the outside, and they are pronounced with a short "a" sound: **ᐊ** a, **ᐸ** pa, **ᑕ** ta, **ᓚ** la.[11]

The overall direction of the chart is sunwise, and the next direction is the grandmother direction, pointing southeast. It is composed of seven ᐊᑖᐦᑭᐯᔩᐦᑲᓇᐠ atâhkipêyîhkanak. The next is the south direction. It is directly on top of the chart, and we have four ᐊᑖᐦᑭᐯᔩᐦᑲᓇᐠ atâhkipêyîhkanak, making the sound **ᐃ,** generally represented by the SRO letter *i*. There are teachings connected to each of the directions, and to the numbers four and seven, and there are laws held within each of the forty-four ᐊᑖᐦᑭᐯᔩᐦᑲᓇᐠ atâhkipêyîhkanak.

These ᐊᑖᐦᑭᐯᔩᐦᑲᓇᐠ atâhkipêyîhkanak are embedded in natural law. They hold the pattern of the little dipper and reflect the

---

11 If you listen to this short video, you can follow along to the sounds of ᐊᑖᐦᑭᐯᔩᐦᑲᓇᐠ atâhkipêyîhkanak, the spirit markers: "Spirit Markers | Nehiyaw Language Video Resource," posted April 29, 2018, by the Centre for Race and Culture Edmonton, *YouTube*, 4 min., 40 sec., www.youtube.com/watch?v=kXpoJ3geugo.

organization of the ᓂᐹᑵᓯᒨᐏᑲᒥᐠ nipâkwêsimôwikamik, the sundance. There are seven stars in the little dipper, and the formation of the little dipper can be found to the right of the ᐊᑖᐦᑭᐯᔩᐦᑲᓇᐠ atâhkipêyîhkanak. It holds the ᐅᒉᐦᑲᑕᕽ ocehkatahk which means martin fisher spirit or north star. You can see how this is illustrated on the front cover of the book. The little dipper represents the ladies' pipe that is used specifically in the ᓂᐹᑵᓯᒨᐏᑲᒥᐠ nipâkwêsimôwikamik, the sundance. The ᐊᑖᐦᑭᐯᔩᐦᑲᓇᐠ atâhkipêyîhkanak have a relationship

with the ethereal. The large ᐊᑖᐦᑭᐯᔩᐦᑲᓇᐠ atâhkipêyîhkanak lie in the grandmother and grandfather directions. The small ᐊᒑᐦᑭᐯᔩᐦᑲᓂᓴᐠ acâhkipêyîhkanisak are on the right side. There are fourteen. I don't know much about the small ᐊᒑᐦᑭᐯᔩᐦᑲᓂᓴᐠ acâhkipêyîhkanisak, but they are the ones that link everything when something needs to be linked.

In each grandfather direction, we have four ᐊᑖᐦᑭᐯᔩᐦᑲᓇᐠ atâhkipêyîhkanak. As I said, the chart begins in the east grandfather direction, on the left side.

ᓚ ᑕ ᐸ ᐊ.

It begins in the east with **ᐊ**. This is the first law, and it makes the sound "a." Its law is ᓵᑮᔩᑐᐠ sâkîyîtok, to love each and one another. The second is **ᐸ**, and it holds the second law and makes the sound "pa." Its law is ᐑᒌᔩᑐᐠ wîcîyitok, to help each and one another. The third is **ᑕ**. It makes the sound "ta," and it marks the third law, ᒦᔪᐚᑕᒧᐠ mîyowâtamok, to have fun, to be joyful. The fourth is **ᓚ**. It makes the sound "la." Its law is ᓲᐦᑲᐢᑖᐧᐠ sôhkastwâk, to make it strong, to be disciplined.

I focus on the first four laws. Because it is enough. Because the number four is important. Maybe curious readers will go out and find them and learn the rest. The chart is symmetrical and numerologically significant. Like I said, four is important – the four directions, east, south, west, north, marked by four ᐊᑖᐦᑭᐯᔩᐦᑲᓇᐠ atâhkipêyîhkanak in each of those directions. There are four ᓂᐹᑫᐧᓯᒨᐃᐧᑲᒥᑲᐧᐦ nipâkwêsimôwikamikwah, sundances, in each cycle.

There are seven ᐊᑖᐦᑭᐯᔩᐦᑲᓇᐠ atâhkipêyîhkanak in each of the grandmother directions (southeast, southwest, northwest, northeast). The number seven is symbolic and significant and practical. Like there are seven holes in our head, seven offerings, seven major tectonic plates on earth. There are many other reasons why the number seven is so important.

The four grandmother directions with their seven ᐊᑖᐦᑭᐯᔩᐦᑲᓇᐠ atâhkipêyîhkanak in each direction make up the number twenty-eight. There are twenty-eight days in a moon cycle. There are thirteen full moons in a lunar year and each of these are our grandmothers. The number thirteen is important for this reason. There are thirteen central plates on a turtle shell.[12] The best way to learn about the turtle's shell is to find a live turtle or its shell.

The offerings are connected to these ᐊᑖᐦᑭᐯᔩᐦᑲᓇᐠ atâhkipêyîhkanak in that they remind us that there are seven offerings that you can give. There are seven offerings, but I don't know the old ᓀᐦᐄᔭᐍᐏᐣ nêhîyawêwin word for offerings, in general.

The first offering is ᐅᐦᒋᑯᐚᐴᐏᐣ ohcikowâpôwin, the most valuable offering – it is the unforced teardrop of gratitude. That's the highest gift. So, when you go into the ᓂᐹᑫᐧᓯᒨᐃᐧᑲᒥᐠ nipâkwêsimôwikamik, the sundance lodge, you hug that tree,

12 The smaller plates around the edge of the turtle shell make the total number of plates twenty-eight.

your tear goes on there. You drop your tear on that, on that sacred tree. It can be in ceremony, but it doesn't have to be. It can happen anywhere. When you feel so grateful, it causes emotions in you and you have that teardrop. That is the best offering. It is good in ceremony, but you can't script that stuff. Well, maybe some people can – pull a hair in your nostril!

The second gift, ᐍᐱᓈᓲᐏᐣ wêpinâsôwin, according to Jerry Saddleback, is the flag or print.

ᐍᐱᓈᓲᐏᓇᐦ wêpinâsôwinah, flags or prints, are brought into ceremony for the ᐅᑮᓯᑰᐘᐠ okîsikôwak, the sacred spirits. There are expectations when one brings these offerings into ceremony. The intent of the person with the ᐍᐱᓈᓲᐏᓇᐦ wêpinâsôwinah is then expressed verbally to the ceremony person. If one can't get to a ceremony, the ᐍᐱᓈᓲᐏᓇᐦ wêpinâsôwinah can be smudged, and the person can express their intentions to nature and to the elements. Having done this, the person then will go tie the ᐍᐱᓈᓲᐏᓇᐦ wêpinâsôwinah to a big straight poplar tree which is slightly tilting to the south. The knot should be to the south of the tree. The prayers are then assisted by the tree and blown throughout the land by the wind. The intentions of that person, expressed in those prayers on those ᐍᐱᓈᓲᐏᓇᐦ wêpinâsôwinah, are then acknowledged by ᐅᒌ,ᐟᒎᐘᐠ okisikôwak, the sacred spirits in the name of the holiest one. That is, those intentions, worries, anxieties are given over to ᐅᑮᓯᑰᐘᐠ okîsikôwak, the sacred spirits, and left there. The person's burden is relieved. This is ᑭᔮᒼ kiyâm. The spirit of ᑭᔮᒼ kiyâm is letting go, and that faith comes from love's form. I say more about this later.

ᒦᔭᐦᑲᓲᐏᐣ mîyahkasôwin or ᐱᑮᐦᑌᓇᒫᐏᐣ pikîhtênamâwin, smudging or smudge, requires a source to begin. Usually, one of the sweetgrasses but not ᐊᒥᐢᑰᐑᐦᑲᐢᐠ amiskôwîhkask, that I know of. In this example, I will use ᒥᐢᑕᑎᒨᐑᐦᑲᐢᐠ

mistatimôwîhkask, horse sweetgrass. ᒥᐢᑕᑎᒨᐑᐦᑲᐢᐠ mistatimôwîhkask is usually picked in mid to late summer. The ᒥᐢᑕᑎᒨᐑᐦᑲᐢᐠ mistatimôwîhkask is picked, cleaned properly, and left to dry. When it has been dried and stored, we use it as ᒦᔭᐦᑲᓯᑲᐣ mîyahkasikan, a smudge. When ready for ceremony, the ᒦᔭᐦᑲᓯᑲᐣ mîyahkasikan, in this case, ᒥᐢᑕᑎᒨᐑᐦᑲᐢᐠ mistatimôwîhkask, is formed into a ball and is lit with ᑲᐢᑲᐢᑭᓭ kaskaskise, a coal or, now, with a match, stove, or lighter.

I once saw my eighty-four-year-old father roll his wheelchair up to the electric stove with his ᒪᐢᑯᓰᔫᐑᐦᑲᐢᐠ maskosîyôwîhkask, sweetgrass on his lap. He turned the element on high. I teased him in a joking way. But he didn't know I was joking when I said, "ᓇᒨᔭᐦ ᐊᓂᒪᐦ ᐁᐓᑯᐦ ᑲᑮ ᐊᐸᒌᐦᑖᔭᐣ namôyah animah ewokoh kakî apacîhtâyan," meaning "you're not supposed to use that [the stove]." And my dad asked me, "ᐊᐑᓇᐦ ᐁᑯᓯᐦ ᐄ ᐃᑘᐟ awînah êkosih î itwet," meaning "who says that?" and I told him, "ᐁᑯᓂᐠ ᑳ ᑭᐢᑫᔩᐦᑕᐦᑭᐠ êkonik kâ kiskeyîhtahkik," meaning "those ones who know the correct ways to do things."

And he said to me, as he lit ᒪᐢᑯᓰᔫᐑᐦᑲᐢᐠ maskosîyôwîhkask on the hot element, "ᐑᔭᐚᐤ ᐁᑯᓯᐦ ᑲ ᐃᑑᑕᒷᐠ wîyawâw êkosih ka itôtamwak," meaning "them, let them do it that way."

What I learned from this is that if we have the tools to do a task, use that tool. It is a matter of pragmatics. I think that is all I want to say about that right now.

After you light the smudge with your ᑲᐢᑲᐢᑭᓭ kaskaskise, coal, ᒦᔭᐦᑲᓯᑲᐣ mîyahkasikan will begin to make smoke. It's like washing your hands. But the element of smoke is going up rather than going down like water. You bring your hands together and draw the smoke between them and around them. Then most people will draw the smoke to their head and purify themselves in that manner. Some people cleanse other important areas on their body with the smoke. So now your being is cleansed. On a practical level, the ritual is very comforting. It allows one to contemplate their relatives and friends and send positive vibes and love to them. One may include specific prayers for individuals and their circumstances. On an ethereal level, the individual is connected to the sacred.

When you smudge an offering like a print, it is cleansed and, through the smoke, infused with your intention and prayer.

The offering of ribbons is ᓭᓂᐹᓇᐦ sênipânah. I don't know much about these ones. Where I come from, the ᓭᓂᐹᓇᐦ sênipânah are used for ᐲᔦᓲᐤ pîyesôw, the thunderbird.

The next offering is ᒦᐦᑭᓰᐦᑲᐦᒋᑲᓂᓴᐦ mîhkisîhkahcikanisah, ornaments made of porcupine quills, say, or hair tufting. I wasn't taught about these.

ᐚᐸᐦᐋᓂᐢ wâpahânis, the little eagle staff that they use in the ᓂᐹᑵᓯᒨᐎᑲᒥᐠ nipâkwêsimôwikamik, the sundance. The little ones there are made of poplar sapling. The poplar sapling is picked and they bend the top of the sapling and tie it to itself with sinew, making a cane-like shape, like the spirit marker ᒋ. And then on that sinew they put four eagle plumes. You can see how valuable these gifts are, because eagle plumes are very hard to get. These are very valuable spiritual offerings. I don't know about the big eagle staff. That is the fifth one. I don't remember the last two. That is all I can say.

Going back to the numbers, there are also twenty-eight spirit markers in the grandmother directions, and there are twenty-eight days in a lunar cycle. In one year, there are thirteen lunar cycles, and we call those moons our grandmothers. ᓅᐦᑯᐨ

nohkom means "my grandmother." When ᐃᐢᑫᐤ iskwêw is going to get her moon time, it is said that her grandmothers are going to be visiting her: ᐄᐐᔫᐦᑯᒥᐟ îwîyohkomit, or she is going to have her grandmothers. Literally, that means "they are with her" – she is infused with and enveloped by the grandmothers.

ᑲᑭᐢᑭᓲᒥᑯᔭᐦ kakiskisomikoyah, this is to remind of us of the four gifts from the grandmothers in the spirit marker chart: they are love, wonder, beauty, amazing. And each grandmother direction in the chart has seven spirit markers and those spirit markers give us our body's directions.

This is how I pass this teaching on in class:

Our first direction is to the left of us, and there, there is love – it is full of wonder, full of beauty, and it is amazing.

Our second direction is in front of us, there are those ones – love, it's full of wonder, it's full of beauty, it's amazing.

Our third direction is to the right of us – there is love, full of wonder, full of beauty, it is amazing.

Our fourth direction is behind us, again there are those ones that will remind us – there is love, full of wonder, full of beauty, it is amazing.

Our fifth direction is below us – there is love, full of wonder, full of beauty, it's amazing.

Our sixth direction is above us – it is love. It is full of wonder, it is full of beauty and it's amazing. Those are the gifts that come from the grandmothers.

The seventh direction is inside us – there are more gifts but this is to remind us that the seventh direction is inside us. That is, inside you, there is love, so you *are* love, it is full of wonder, so you *are* wonderful, it is full of beauty, so you *are* beautiful, it's amazing, so you *are* amazing.

There are different ways of doing those. This is how I do it. And so, it is believed that those gifts are there irrespective of our own personal opinions, these gifts our grandmothers gave us. The thing I like about them, these gifts, they can't be refuted. When you tell someone they are amazing, it can't be refuted. But sometimes it's what we do in our mind – we negate these gifts. But from the perspective of ᓀᐦᐄᔭᐤ nêhîyaw those gifts are from spirit, from the grandmothers. They are irrefutable.

One way we learned to remember the whole orientation of the chart, the grandmother and grandfather directions, was by actually making the sounds of the spirit markers while facing in each direction. This was shown to us by Deneh'Cho Thompson. In this way, with each spirit marker, with each sound, with each law, we reoriented ourselves to the land. This is how we did it:

Reader,
face south and put your chart on the floor. When we are working with the chart, our orientation is always to the south. We always face the south.
To the left is east.
Face the east and speak the first four ᐊᑖᐦᑭᐯᔩᐦᑲᓇᐠ atâhkipêyîhkanak.
Starting with ᐊ a and moving from the right to the left, from the inside to outside, to the east: ᒐ ᑕ ᐸ ᐊ.
This is the first grandfather direction.

Then you face the southeast in that grandmother direction and speak the next seven ᐊᑖᐦᑭᐯᔩᐦᑲᓇᐠ atâhkipêyîhkanak.

Then you face south in the grandfather direction and you speak the next four ᐊᑖᐦᑭᐯᔩᐦᑲᓇᐠ atâhkipêyîhkanak.

Then you face southwest in the grandmother direction and you speak the next seven ᐊᑖᐦᑭᐯᔩᐦᑲᓇᐠ atâhkipêyîhkanak.

Then you face west in the grandfather direction and you speak those four ᐊᑖᐦᑭᐯᔩᐦᑲᓇᐠ atâhkipêyîhkanak.

Then you face northwest in the grandmother direction there and speak those next seven ᐊᑖᐦᑭᐯᔩᐦᑲᓇᐠ atâhkipêyîhkanak.

Then you face north in the grandfather direction and speak those four ᐊᑖᐦᑭᐯᔩᐦᑲᓇᐠ atâhkipêyîhkanak.

For the last seven grandmother direction, you face the northeast and then speak those ᐊᑖᐦᑭᐯᔩᐦᑲᓇᐠ atâhkipêyîhkanak.
There are forty-four ᐊᑖᐦᑭᐯᔩᐦᑲᓇᐠ atâhkipêyîhkanak in total.

This is what Deneh'Cho gave us. When we face east, we speak the east ᐊᑖᐦᑭᐯᔩᐦᑲᓇᐠ atâhkipêyîhkanak out loud. When we face the southeast grandmother direction we speak ᐊᑖᐦᑭᐯᔩᐦᑲᓇᐠ atâhkipêyîhkanak out loud and so on. This is how we reorient ourselves to the land with ᐋᑖᐦᑭᐯᔩᐦᑲᓇᐠ atâhkipêyîhkanak, the spirit markers, and the chart.

ᐋ is the supreme being.
ᐋᔩᐢ âyîs means "us," the diminutive of spirit, the diminutive of the supreme being, the people are a diminutive of ᐋ â.

ᐋᔩᓰᔩᓇᐤ[13] âyîsîyînaw: human beings are made by the supreme being.
All of us are ᐋᔩᐢ âyîs, the six nations, all of us,
we are ᐋᔩᐢ âyîs.

Okay, now from there we come here through those elements.

ᐄᔩ îyî, from ᐄᔩᓇᐤ îyînaw, is the morpheme for ᐄᔩᑯᐲᐄᐤ îyîkopîwîw, fog or mist, and that is where we all come from. ᐄᔩᑯᐲᐄᐤ îyîkopîwîw is that mist we come from, that mist, that fog, the earth's fog, but those elements are what were used to mould us, and that is ᐄᐄᒉᐢᑰᐘᑭᓂᑯᔭᕽ îwîcêskôwakinikoyahk.

Like I said, this is how the supreme being brought us to this earth. ᐄᐄᒉᐢᑰᐘᑭᓂᑯᔭᕽ îwîcêskôwakinikoyahk, this is the moulding of the two-legged people from the elements.

Water exists in three states, solid, liquid, and gas (mist).

We were made with those elements. So, that is why I was thinking that word, ᐄᐄᒉᐢᑰᐘᑭᓂᑯᔭᕽ îwîcêskôwakinikoyahk is so important, because of the elements what we are moulded from. And we came in from that mist.

ᐋᔩᐦᐊᐩ âyîhay is one person's expression of gratitude to another person. In today's English terms, it would be "thank you." In ᓀᐦᐄᔭᐍᐏᐣ nêhîyawêwin, giving thanks is also rooted in the creator. In ᓀᐦᐄᔭᐤ nêhîyaw that word there, it includes the supreme being, ᐋ â. It is two people recognizing that one person is giving gratitude to the other person saying, "you, you've given

13 When the the context is more serious, the first spirit marker vowel sound is long: ᐋ; when it is less so, the spirit marker vowel sound is short: ᐊ.

me this. I'm grateful and I'm grateful in ᐋ â's name." Do you get that a little bit?

Now, I hate to keep being repetitive, but I'm going to be repetitive here to say that when they use ᐋ â, what they're actually saying is, "with creator's blessing" or "in creator's name." This would be understood in many societies around the world as "with god's blessing" or in "god's name." And they say ᐋ â a lot in ceremony, but a lot of old people, when they used to meet me, they'd say, "ᐋ â, reuben, ᐋ â, reuben." And I didn't realize they were saying, "in the holiness's presence," "in the creator's name." Yeah, like, they've come upon something, like, if I came upon you and I'm surprised and I'm happy, I say, "ᐋ â, ᓃᑎᒼ nîtim."

This is an example of what I mean when I say about ᓀᐦᐄᔭᐍᐏᐣ nêhîyawêwin, that the language moves in idea. The idea of ᐋ â is the idea of gratitude, the idea of love. But not just the idea, the actual spirit of ᐋ â, the being of ᐋ â. This is what I have been led to understand, the supreme being moves through the human. The supreme being gave us that breath and in that breath is our dna and ᓀᐦᐄᔭᐍᐏᐣ nêhîyawêwin.

Where ᐋ â is there are no stars, there are no galaxies, there are no black holes, there are no supernovas, and yet if you put all of the stars in the universe together, they would not have all of the light that ᐋ â has, and that light is generated by ᓵᑮᔩᑑᐏᐣ sâkîyîtôwin, love.

painting by Kaitlyn Purcell

The first spirit marker ᐊ a is the first law, ᓵᑮᔩᑐᐠ sâkîyîtok, to love each and one another.

"If you get this first law, the others will fall into place." That's what my brother, Carl Quinn, says.

We are talking about the east direction and the different ways the sun comes up, the different places that the sun comes up, and the way that is celebrated and understood throughout the year. Love is the first law, it comes from the fourth dimension. It is the fourth level of communication. There are four levels of communication. I talk about these levels of communication in class.

ᐄᑭᐢᑭᓱᒥᑯᔭᕽ îkiskisomikoyahk, the land, it reminds us and shows us what ᓵᑮᔩᑐᐏᐣ sâkîyîtôwin is by ᓵᑭᐸᑳᐤ sâkipakâw. ᓵᑭᐸᑳᐤ sâkipakâw is when the grass is coming, the grass is coming out of the ground, the green unfurling, coming into view from the bosom of the earth. That green grass, the unfurling leaves, all plant life coming forth – that is ᓵᑭᐸᑳᐤ sâkipakâw and love is the interconnectedness of trees in the spring or at the time of blooming, leafing, unfurling. ᓵᑮᔩᑑᐏᐣ sâkîyîtôwin and ᓵᑭᐸᑳᐤ sâkipakâw share an important morpheme and that morpheme is ᓵᑭ sâki.

To remind each other about love, of earth love, the way the earth, our mother ᑭᑳᐑᔨᓇᐤᐊᐢᑮᐩ[14] kikâwîyinaw-askîy, loves us more than we can know.

So, there is an important relationship between love and the springtime. How the world comes into being, it comes into being seen, unfurling, ᓵᑫᐍ sâkêwê.

14 The old people said it this way.

ᓵᑫᐍ sâkêwê means "to come into view," and this is part of the processing of spring, and spring is a form of earth love, to see and to be seen.

And so, love is embedded in natural law. Natural law plays out in the natural rhythms of the year, the moon phases. These are the natural cycles that organize people's cultural and spiritual lives. Like the way people would look to the epoch. Like in the autumnal equinox you would make your promise and then revisit it in winter solstice. Your final commitment would be made in the vernal equinox and then acted out in the summer solstice. ᐊᓱᒋᑫ asocikê, you promise, you make a promise, and then that promise is revisited at winter solstice. By the spring you cement your purpose. And then in summer you act on that – you learn a song, you learn some ᓀᐦᐄᔭᐤ nêhîyaw phrases. You may commit to feeding people at a ceremony. Or you may commit to visiting more ᑮᐦᑌᐊᔭᐠ kîhtêayak, elders. You may commit to fasting.

ᓵᑭᐸᑳᐤ sâkipakâw, spring budding.

The most important event, I think. What do you think?

ᓵᑭᐸᑳᐤ sâkipakâw, not spring necessarily, but when the grass comes up. What do you call it, foliage? I want you to talk about it, ᓃᑎᒼ nîtim. The similarities of ᐃᐢᑫᐤ iskwêw being with child and giving birth, and the similarities between that and ᓵᑭᐸᑳᐤ sâkipakâw. You can see when ᐃᐢᑫᐤ iskwêw is with child and then throughout the winter you see the growth in her belly. I think there is a similarity in that, when the baby comes into view, what happens to the mother and the community, that tender emotion, that love is part of ᓵᑮᔩᑑᐃᐧᐣ sâkîyîtôwin.

ᑭᐢᑯᐦᐊᐚᓲᐤ kikiskohawâsôw – the child is cloaked in the placenta, ᐃᐢᑫᐤ iskwêw is cloaked in the child. That child is ᐅᒫᓂᑌᐤ omânitew, a guest from the stars.[15]

ᓵᑭᐸᑳᐤ sâkipakâw – is when the earth does all that, the smells, the sights, the eye stimulation, and what that does to our brains. This is the world view. That is why I am so stuck on this world view.

Each ᓀᐦᐄᔭᐤ nêhîyaw word is a thesis. Each word needs to be researched. What does it really mean? Each word needs a whole chapter to describe it, and we need to always be mindful of the context. What was the context? What was the time? What was the "right now" of that word? ᒣᑳᐧᐨ mêkwâc, right now. Context is always so important. That is, the time is important. When did it happen? What was the season when it happened? This is important so that the message is understood – filled with meaning. Each ᓀᐦᐄᔭᐍᐏᐣ nêhîyawêwin word is contextualized within a web of relations, a network of ethereal, spiritual, and practical dimensions.

Our language is linked to the land. It is the language of this land. The land shows us that, and as we see in the spring, ᓵᑮᔩᑑᐏᐣ sâkîyîtôwin or love occurs. Those flowers change dimension from the seed. So, they live out this life and continue to permeate the land and to attract other relatives to them: insect people,

15 We come to this earth as ᐊᒐᐦᑯᐢ acahkos, stardust, and as such we cloak and suffuse our mothers with our essence. At that moment of our conception, our mothers are transformed. This is what happens when ᐃᐢᑫᐘᐠ iskwêwak are with child, ᐄᑭᐢᑯᐦᐊᐚᓱᐟ î kiskohawâsot. And when those children have just arrived, they are understood as ᐅᒫᓂᑌᐤ omânitew, guests. If you look at the morpheme ᒫᓂmâni, then you can see its connection to ᒪᓂᑑᐤ manitôw and understand that this baby is a creative force that transforms those with whom it visits. And in this worldview, all guests who come visiting are themselves a creative force.

winged people, two-legged people, four-leggeds, and water relatives. And the next year that cycle is going to happen again, as long as the sun shines.

For ᐊᑖᐦᑭᐯᔩᐦᑲᓇᐠ atâhkipêyîhkanak, the spirit markers, as they are written out in the chart, love is the first teaching.

And this is also connected to what we mean when we say, "all my relations." In this we understand ourselves in relation to all things and beings.

It was in 1997, when I went to that place, Kanehsatà:ke, and had a pipe ceremony with the local Kanien'kehá:ka Mohawk elder (ᑮᐦᑌᐊᔭᐦ kîhtêayah) John Cree. He talked about their ceremonial activities while they were being held under occupation by la Sûreté du Québec and then, subsequently, the Canadian Armed Forces. He spoke about the ᐅᑮᓯᑰᐤ okîsikôw, a sacred spirit, ᔫᑎᐣ yôtin, and then gave us a teaching specifically about ᐲᓯᒼ pîsim, the sun. One of the things that I was told about this relationship, by that man who told me, is this: "there is one who comes up, there is a door in the east, byᑮᐦᒋᑲᒥᐠ kîhcikamik, the great water there, there is one that comes up there every day, and we call it a grandfather, and it travels the sky, and it says, 'Everything I touch I am related to,' and then it sets towards the other door, west, at ᑮᐦᒋᑲᒥᐠ kîhcikamik, the great water there. So, it rises and sets upon this land." So, that is what he said, and what I got out of that is, ᐲᓯᒼ ᑭᒧᓲᒥᓇᐤ pîsim kimosôminaw, the sun, our grandfather, rises and sets upon the land. Well, in a relational way, and I started thinking about symbiosis and photosynthesis and how the old people from Saddle Lake, from treaty 6 territory, would say that everything is related. Even the roots, from the plants and the trees, communicate from one end of this continent to the other through an underground network, and all kinds of things they teach us. Like, when it is most opportune for the trees to let their ᐲᐄᐧᔭᐦ pîwîyah, seeds, go into the winds. The wind is our relative as well, and so the elements come into play. So many things, the land and the wind.

So, that was John Cree. He said he was a Mohawk. He joked, "I am in charge of all the Cree people." "My name is John Cree," he said. He was a funny guy. Kinda like that dry humour, eh. So, he got me thinking about how we are all related, every one of us in the six nations. It got me thinking about symbiosis and the root systems and the time of ᓵᑭᐸᑳᐤ sâkipakâw, the spring budding time.

ᓵᑭᐸᑳᐤ sâkipakâw, the trees are budding, it is the time of grass growing and leaf budding. But for me those words, like budding, don't really work. It is an emergence of ᓵᑮᔩᑐᐃᐧᐣ sâkîyîtowin from the earth, a coming into view.

ᓵᑫᐁᐧᐤ sâkêwêw – coming into view, she shows herself
ᐯ pe – come over
ᐱᒼ pim – life
Like the bear shows itself in the spring, ᐯ ᓵᑫᐁᐧᐤ pe sâkêwêw
ᐊᐢᑮᐩ ᐅᑕᐚᓯᒥᓴᐦ ᐯ ᓵᑫᐁᐧᐊᐧᐠ
askîy otawâsimisa pê sâkêwêwak
the earth's children are coming into view

ᓵᑭᐸᑳᐤ
sâkipakâw, all the plants coming into view, unfurling
Photosynthesis as love – how the sun is in relation with the plants and the plants with the sun and in each other.

Spring is a time when the earth expresses her love. Energy comes out of the earth. The buds unfurl. The earth comes into view. This coming into view is a form of earth-love. And the etymology of the word ᓵᑮᔩᑐᐃᐧᐣ sâkîyitowin, for love, is ᓵᑭ

sâki, coming out – ᐯ ᓵᑫᐍᐤ pe sâkêwêw. That is a specific thing coming into view, a bear, a blade of grass, coming into view. You see them coming towards you. You see them coming out. I'm not a linguist, but that is how I understand it – in ᓀᐦᐄᔭᐍᐏᐣ nêhîyawêwin, love is etymologically connected to spring, to coming into view, to seeing and to being seen, ᓵᑮᔩᑐᕽ sâkîyîtok.

To see. To be seen. To come into view. To be loved by the earth. The earth shows us enveloping, practical love. After that anything goes!

The connection between us is holy.
The connection illuminates the holy.
The idea of love being "that which emanates from you."
ᓵᑭᐸᑳᐤ sâkipakâw

The bear emanates.
The bush emanates.
Everything coming out. The earth first and then the animals – they come into their plumage. That love is so paramount, and we enter into a relationship with that love, remembering the first law.

ᒦᔪᐢᑲᒥᐣ mîyoskamin is spring, the time for ᓵᑭᐸᑳᐤ sâkipakâw.

And spring budding brings ᐱᒫᑎᓲᐏᐣ pimâtisôwin.

Having listened to my brother, Carl, who studied ᓀᐦᐄᔭᐍᐏᐣ nêhîyawêwin, I learned that each of these morphemes has meaning, like ᓴ sa and like ᐱᒼ pim.

ᐱᒼ pim means "life's movement."

ᐱᒧᐦᑌ pimohtê – most people will translate that as "walk." However, as ᐱᒼ pim means "life's movement," and ᐱᒧᐦᑌ pimohtê literally means “life’s movement on the land.” Or ᐱᒥᐦᐋ pimihâ, that’s movement in the air. Like the birds. How they move there. ᐱᒥᐦᐋ pimihâ, that’s their life’s movement in the air. So, ᐱᒼ pim means “life movement” and ᐱᒧᐦᑌ pimohtê means “life’s movement on the land,” and ᐱᒥᐦᐋ pimihâ (ᐱᒼ pim) means “life’s movement in the air.” Like the birds when they do that, that is ᐱᒥᐦᐋ pimihâ or flying. When you talk about what these relatives are doing, those winged ones, that is where their life is, in that realm. And others as well, like microorganisms.

We talked about that contract between the trees and the wind and the trees move that and it gives us life. And ᐱᒥᒋᒣ pimicimê, that is life’s movement on the water, in the water, life’s movement on the water. A lot of people think it means swimming or floating on the water, but it has to do with life again, life’s movement. There, if we look at who is constantly moving – ᐱᒥᒋᒣ pimicimê, swimming, and whoever has to do with the water. Whether it’s the duck swimming, or the fish, or the beaver, whoever it is, it is life’s movement in the water. That’s ᐱᒥᒋᒣ pimicimê.

Like ᒫᑲᐧ mâkwa, the loon, or ᐊᒥᐢᐠ amisk, the beaver, extending its life force, swimming, the energy from the body is transferred into the water, the energy ripples out into the water. When they’re going, their life’s course is going. You can see that their life’s force is expanding, flowing, as they move as well. Whoever it is. This is ᐱᒥᒋᒣ pimicimê, life’s movement with the water. It’s going through that. So, ᐱᒼ pim, in this example, has to do with life moving in the water.

And here when we look at who is moving constantly, there is ᔫᑎᐣ yôtin, and there’s also a twin for you, then. And that’s ᐋᔩᐚᐢᑎᐣ âyîwâstin, the absolute calm. It’s complete, total calm. This comes to us every once in a while. When there’s absolutely no bird, no insect, nothing moving. Not a leaf is blowing – absolute calm. That's a very powerful place to be in. That has its life's movement, also. It is completely totally calm, but still there is ᐱᒫᑎᓲᐃᐧᐣ pimâtisôwin in there. And in that place of ᐋᔩᐋᐧᐢᑎᐣ âyîwâstin on ᐊᐢᑮᐩ askîy, the land, what we do is called ᐱᒧᐦᑌ pimohtê.

Because when you talk about these descriptions of what these species do, what these relatives are doing, these winged ones there, that's where their life takes place, their lives takes place, in that realm, bound in their own loving environment, which is what we all do. We are all bound to our environments. Be it air, land, or water. Yeah, on this ᒪᐦᐄᐦᑲᐣ ᒣᐢᑲᓇᐤ mahîhkan meskanaw, wolf's trail. We talked about the contract between the trees and the wind, how the trees supply oxygen. How the contract between the wind and the trees brings about an exchange of necessity. The wind moves that. So, it gives us life. And you get all kinds of different chemicals from that wind, when it's moving on the land. Just like today, there's a little breeze, a little tiny breeze out there – that is ᐱᒼ pim.

And love envelops ᐱᒼ pim.

In two-legged people relationships, I was told that we need four things: love, honour, trust, and respect. These qualities are like workers, supporting life. For us humans, anyway, there's so many things attached to that love. There's the other side of love, and that is fear. And fear has its envy, jealousy, suspicion, and other things like that, things that work against life. But if we enter into that relationship with just love, respect, honour, trust, those tentacles of suspicion, jealousy, anger, revenge, vengeance, things like that, we can just let those go – if we are willing to do so.

Love, honour, trust and respect. You always have to have those four things. I was told. Any relationship, whether it be intimate, familial, or social, whether it be a relationship with the plant people or the four-legged people, this is ᐚᐦᑯᐦᑑᐃᐧᐣ wâhkohtôwin. So, we just take that love in. We know there's going to be other things, like crazy things, happening. You know, like energy-sucking things. But the love is going to remain constant. It's not going to drag us. That's actually the one that's going to give us the strength. Those other tentacles that, you know, worry, anxiety, those things like that, that we attach to love. But love is the emanating of tender emotion, good will, positive vibes, and love. Yeah, positive vibes. That's what love is, sending those positive vibes. That is ᑳᑮᔨᓯᒨᐃᐧᐣ kâkîyisimôwin, when you use your voice to express your prayer.

Letting it go. I said that lots of times before, ᑭᔮᒼ kiyâm, letting it go.

ᑭᔮᒼ kiyâm means "letting go," trusting in a power beyond our own, and being quiet in that letting go, to quiet yourself and let things go. It's kind of a meditative state. The word ᑭᔮᒼ kiyâm is related to the word ᑭᔮᒪᐱᐦ kiyâmapih. ᐊᐱ api is in there too, to sit. To sit in that state of meditative quiet, ᑭᔮᒪᐱᐦ kiyâmapih, to let everything go.

When you're doing that, you're giving all of the worries and cares over to the supreme being, or to that first law, ᓵᑮᔩᑐᐃᐧᐣ sâkîyîtowin, love. When you sit in that state, you're giving your cares over to some ethereal force, and you say, "whatever's gonna happen, ᑭᔮᒼ kiyâm." Where this is most evident is when people go and fast, go and dance at the ᓂᐹᑫᐧᓯᒨᐃᐧᑲᒥᐠ nipâkwêsimôwikamik, the sundance, and take on self-sacrificing – going without food and water – what they're saying is, "to heck with it, whatever happens, happens," and that means anything from you're gonna receive the greatest blessing, or maybe you're even gonna die, but you've accepted whatever. When you're going into that fast, or you're going without food and water – you're accepting whatever is happening, as that's the way things are going to be, according to ᐋ â. ᑭᔮᒼ kiyâm.

Infused into ᓀᐦᐃᔭᐍᐏᐣ nêhîyawêwin are meanings, connections, and teachings about the world we live in and about how we might live.

This includes a commitment to be vulnerable, a commitment to be open, a commitment to be reciprocal.

ᑮᓯᑳᐤ kîsikâw.

And ᑮᓯᑳᐤ, the day, love is evident in the day – ᑮᓯᑳᐤ kîsikâw is often translated into English as "day," but that is just the surface layer of the word. It radiates with deeper meanings and connections: ᑮᓯᑳᐤ kîsikâw is connected to ᐅᑮᓯᑰᐤ okîsikôw, sacred spirit. When the orb is in the sky, it rises in the east and sets in the west; it is an event caused by ᐅᑮᓯᑰᐤ okîsikôw, sacred spirit. It is a spiritual event, a movement, a moment of spiritual illumination. So, in ᓀᐦᐃᔭᐍᐏᐣ nêhîyawêwin we don't call it "day," but a spiritual moment.

ᐅᑮᓯᑰᐤ okîsikôw, sacred spirit, also illuminates the word ᐅᑮᓯᑰᐤ okîsikôw.

ᐅᑮᓯᑰᐤ okîsikôw is a sacred spirit. Like one that looks after ᓂᐲᕀ nipîy, ᐲᔦᓲᐤ pîyesôw is ᐅᑮᓯᑰᐤ okîsikôw. ᔫᑎᐣ yôtin, the wind, is also ᐅᑮᓯᑰᐤ okîsikôw.

And ᒥᐢᑮᓯᐠ miskîsik and ᒥᐢᑮᓯᑿᐦ miskîsikwah are the words for eyeball and eyeballs. The morpheme ᑮᓯᐠ kîsik, sacred spirit, that is the foundation for the word "eyeball." In ᓀᐦᐃᔭᐍᐏᐣ nêhîyawêwin, the understanding is that we view the world from that foundation. ᒥᐢᑮᓯᑿᐦ miskîsikwah helps us connect to the spirit. From that foundation there are instructions on how we are to perceive ᐱᒫᑎᓲᐏᐣ pimâtisôwin.

And it is ᑮᓯᐠ kîsik in those sockets – ᒥᐢᑮᓯᐠ miskîsik and ᒥᐢᑮᓯᑿᐦ miskîsikwah. This has implications for how we view the world, how we're told to see the day.

We see the day as a spiritual event through ᒥᐢᑮᓯᑿᐦ miskîsikwah, eyes.

The eyes allow us to see all that is sacred.

What is sacred? Everything. Where is sacred? Everywhere.

Our grandfather comes from the east through a doorway from the great waters there, travels through the sky. As he travels, he says, "everything I touch, I'm related to. I'm related to that." This one is ᐅᑭᒫᐤ ᑮᓯᐠ okimâw kîsik, the leader spirit, ᐲᓯᒼ pîsim, the sun. On a personal level, we all observe life through these two balls in there, those eyeballs, we call these ᒥᐢᑮᓯᑿᐦ miskîsikwah – and spirit is attached to this word.

So, in ᓀᐦᐃᔭᐍᐏᐣ nêhîyawêwin, ᐲᓯᒼ pîsim is often translated as "sun." The sun is actually ᑮᓯᑳᐏᐲᓯᒼ kîsikâwipîsim (some people say "day sun") and the moon is ᑎᐱᐢᑳᐃᐲᓯᒼ tipiskâwipîsim (some say "night sun"). The word "sun," is not an accurate translation of the word ᐲᓯᒼ pîsim.

ᑮᓯᐢ **kîsik** – sacred spirit
ᑮᓯᑳᐤ **kîsik**âw – the illumination of the sacred spirit (daytime)
ᐅᑮᓯᑰᐤ o**kîsik**ôw – a specific sacred spirit
ᑮᓯᑰᐤ **kîsik**ôw – a general sacred spirit
ᒥᐢᑮᓯᐢ mis**kîsik** (eyeball) – given us to perceive spirit or the sacred
ᒥᐢᑮᓯᑲᐧᐦ mis**kîsik**wah (eyeballs) – our sacred spirit finders

Often, ᒥᐢᑮᓯᑲᐧᐦ miskîsikwah is translated as "eyes," ᒥᐢᑮᓯᐢ miskîsik as "eyeball," and ᑮᓯᑳᐤ kîsikâw translated as "day." In my studies, I have found that these translations are insufficient, because our eyes hold the sacred spirit. The day holds the sacred spirit. Our eyes are like the day infused with the light of the sacred spirit. Natural law can be seen in these words.

I would say it's the illumination. ᑮᓯᑲᐤ kîsikâw, this is the illumination of the sacred, illumination of sacredness. Yeah, illumination of the sacred spirit, ᑮᓯᑲᐤ kîsikâw. ᒥᐢᑮᓯᐢ miskîsik, that's the one I have a problem with, eyes. We need to translate that, succinctly. ᒥᐢᑮᓯᐢ miskîsik it is just one, it helps us to see that, the spirit and everything, because it's illuminated. So, this one looks for that illumination. So how do you say that it looks to that illumination? Looks to what's being illuminated? See, it's the other way around, eh. It serves a different function than what you would think in western ideologies. So, I don't know how to say that. It is supposed to help, it's given to us by ᐋ â to help detect the spirit. It looks towards the illumination. It looks to find the illumination. I think this flows good, ᑮᓯᐢ **kîsik**, ᑮᓯᑳᐤ **kîsik**âw, ᐅᑮᓯᑰᐤ o**kîsik**ôw, ᑮᓯᑰᐤ**kîsik**ôw, ᒥᐢᑮᓯᐢ mis**kîsik**, ᒥᐢᑮᓯᑲᐧᐦ mis**kîsik**wah flows very well, helping people understand, or at least getting people to think, eh. And the idea of doing something like this, I was told, is to help people to think, to remind each other. That's what the old people always told us in the circles, "ᑭᐢᑭᓱᒥᑐᐠ kiskisomitok, remind each other!" They would speak to us with authority – "ᐲᑭᐢᑳᐧᑎᑐᐠ

pîkiskwâtitok, talk to each other." The old people would kind of raise their voices and talk about respecting yourself – they are raising their voices trying to incite people to think in a different way. Colonialism silenced many people. Such deafening silence. And some people never forgot. And more people are coming out now, that is what I like.

And every one of us needs to listen with three ears, to understand, and listening should include ᓇᓇᐦᐄᐦᑕᐚᑲᔦ nanahîhtawakaye, the heart. This literally means "listen with your ear." But it asks us to listen with ᓇᓇᐦᐄᐦᑕᐚᑲᔦ nanahîhtawakaye, our third ear. And what I was told was that the ear and the heart share a resemblance. The three levels of understanding often come with listening not only with our physical ears and intellectual mind, but there is understanding that occurs when we listen with our hearts. That is what I am told, anyways.

ᐸ

ᐑᒌᔩᑐᐠ wîcîyitok

the second law, help each and one another

painting by Kaitlyn Purcell

ᐐᒌᔩᑑᐠ wîcîyitok, the second law, help each and one another. How you will likely hear it now is without the ᔩ yi. Those syllables are often not used. You are likely to hear ᐐᒌᑑᐠ wîcî'tok. So those laws are not expressed there so fully anymore when those syllables are missing. Those beings are missing, those footprints are gone from that word.

So, we can help each other remember those syllables, those ᐊᑖᐦᑭᐯᔩᐦᑲᓇᐠ atâhkipêyîhkanak, remind each other, helping each and one another.

ᐐᒌᔩᑑᐠ wîcîyitok is connected to ᐐᓱᐦᑲᒫᑐᐏᐣ wîsohkamâtowin, helping each other, assisting each other, and ᒪᒥᓰᑐᑖᑐᐏᐣ mamisîtotâtowin , depending on each other, helping people understand and remember the ᓀᐦᐃᔭᐤ nêhîyaw world view.

The ᓀᐦᐃᔭᐤ nêhîyaw world view is animate.

All things made animate are spirits or have spirits.

In the *Online Cree Dictionary*[16] this is the translation for "east wind:" "it is an east wind; there is a wind blowing all night into the morning ᐚᐸᓃᔪᐍᐤ wâpanîyowêw."

It is an east wind or "there is a wind blowing all night into the morning." But it should be *the wind – the wind* is blowing all night into the morning. The ᐍᐤ wêw makes it animate, that is, someone is doing the action. So, it should be "*the* wind is

16 *Nehiyaw Masinahikan Online Cree Dictionary*, www.creedictionary .com. I was first made aware of this word by my brother Carl.

blowing all night into the morning" – "the" because *someone* is doing it. It is animate – someone, the wind, is doing it.

It would take a chapter to explain each word, and you would always need to be thinking about its context. The "right now" ᒣᑳᐨ mêkwâc of that word. I want to talk about the world view. In that world view, in that world, ᐚᐸᓃᔪᐍᐤ wâpanîyowêw means someone is there.

That someone is animate.

That someone is ᐲᓯᒼ pîsim, the sun.

That someone is ᔫᑎᐣ yôtin, the wind.

ᔫᑎᐣ yôtin, the wind, is so important in the ᓀᐦᐄᔭᐤ nêhîyaw mindset. Brings us oxygen from the trees. ᔫᑎᐣ yôtin, the wind, blew the stardust onto the earth to make us. We come from stardust. It is why we are here.

ᑭᐢᑭᓅᐘᐦᐊᒫᑯᓲᐎᐣ[17] kiskinôwahamâkôsôwin means "education."

And you know, this what I'm trying to do. ᑭᐢᑭ kiski is to remember. ᑭᐢᑭᓅᐘᐦᐊᒫᑯᓲᐎᐣ kiskinôwahamâkôsôwin to remember for yourself, that is what it means. It means to attend to the details of what is happening in whatever context it is: learning, learning about picking berries, learning about whatever it is. Like, if you give me a fish, I'll eat for a day. But if you teach me how to fish, I'm going to watch you. I'm going to observe. I'm going to remember and do that – ᑭᐢᑭ kiski. I'm going to be observing your facial features as you fish and whatever. And I'm going to take into account what you do with the nets and how you harvest all these things. So, what you are

17 ᑭᐢᑭᓅᐘᐦᐊᒫᑰᓲᐎᐣ is an alternative spelling example.

doing as ᑭᐢᑭᓄᐦᐊᒫᑫᐤ kiskinohamâkew, the teacher, you are being the legend, the map there, and I am the student, you know. It makes it sound like I'm teaching myself. But I'm teaching myself by observing you. I'm observing you. And that's how I learn from that paradigm.

And it has the word for the medicine wheel in there – ᑭᐢᑯᓅᐋᐧᒌᐦᒋᑲᐣ kiskônôwâcîhcikan. The understanding of the medicine wheel is in there in that morpheme. And it is connected with the fourth law, ᓀᐦᑲᐢᑖᐧ sôhkastwâ, taking strength, learning strength from other beings. So, you are the map. So, there's lots of maps, legends, or teachers. You get to be engaged with ᒫᒪᐢᑳᐨ mâmaskâc, wonder. And when I think of that when the leaves are coming out and enjoying those and even with the caterpillars becoming cocoons and then butterflies, that's ᒪᒫᐦᑖᐤ mamâhtâw, that's amazing. Yeah. That's ᒪᒫᐦᑖᐤ mamâhtâw, amazing, children being born. That's ᒪᒫᐦᑖᐤ mamâhtâw, amazing. So, there's so much to be amazed about. The land, the air, how it flows differently all the time. There the little green leaves are unfurling. Yes, out of branches in the early spring, that if you didn't look carefully, would seem inanimate.

All these different legends, these different maps, will teach you how to survive, how to be, and be well.

And that chart, it is ᑭᐢᑯᓅᐋᐧᒌᐦᒋᑲᐣ kiskonôwâcîhcikan, a medicine wheel, just as much as those ones you see on the plains, and each spirit marker is part of that legend, filled with the meaning of life. From its perspective, right. Those ᐊᑖᐦᑭᐯᔩᐦᑲᓇᐠ atâhkipêyîhkanak, spirit markers, are truly a legend, like a map. It tells us where we came from. Where we are going and where we are on ᒪᐦᐄᐦᑲᐣ ᒣᐢᑲᓇᐤ mahîhkan meskanaw, the wolf's trail, the Milky Way, and that was before technology and telescopes and things like that. ᒥᐢᑕᒣᒫᑲᓇᐠ

mistamêmâkanak, the ancestors, followed the stars and that was their guiding way, but that star chart was also a guiding way for them. I like the way they have the same name – the stars and spirit markers – ᐊᒐᕽ acâhk, ᐋᒑᐦᑭᐯᔩᐦᑲᓂᐢ acâhkipêyîhkanis, ᐊᒐᕽ acâhk, ᐊᑖᕽ atâhk, ᐊᑖᐦᑭᐯᔩᐦᑲᐣ atâhkipêyîhkan.

The suffix ᐯᔩᐦᑲᐣ peyîhkan – that means "a marker" and ᐊᑖᕽ atâhk is always spirit and ᐊᒐᕽ acâhk is a small spirit. That chart is a legend.

So, I look at that chart as it was shown to us children in 1971, and it has so much meaning as far as directions are concerned – the grandfather and the grandmother directions.

Anyways, I was saying that the chart, it's truly a legend. As you know. ᒥᐢᑕᒣᒫᑲᓇᕁ mistamêmâkanak, the ancestors, followed the stars. ᐊᑖᐦᑭᐯᔩᐦᑲᓇᕁ atâhkipêyîhkanak, the spirit markers, are an embodiment of their world view – through them ᓀᐦᐃᔭᐍᐏᐣ nêhîyawêwin holds this world view.

Do everything out of love instead of fear. Fear wants to have dominance over things and others. Fear wants to envelop you. Love transforms.

painting by Kaitlyn Purcell

Following the third law, ᒦᔭᐚᑕᒧᐠ let's feel joy, let's enjoy life!

These are instructions on how to live.

This is from my uncle, who was a warrior. I don't know if it's called a poem. I don't think so. You can tell me what it is. He wrote this:

"What that is above, it is powerful. What that is below, it is powerful. The earth is my home."

I think that is so beautiful. That is my uncle Charles, Charles Gladue, a soldier in WW II, my dad's brother.

My dad said once, as we were walking by someone who I felt sorry for in the moment, "ᑮᐢᐱᐣ ᐁᑳ ᑮᑲᐧᐩ ᑮ ᐄᔩᑑᑕᒪᐚᐤ ᐋᔩᓰᔩᓇᐤ ᑳᔭ ᑯᓂᑕ kîspin ekâ kîkway kî îyitôtamawâw âyîsîyînaw kâya konita."

If you are walking by someone and you feel pity, if you can't do something for that person, don't do it for nothing (don't perform pity for pity's sake).

We too were living in that rough time. This helped me come to terms with the fact that if I can't help a person, someone else will. That person lives according to the supreme being, as does everyone. I am not the centre of that person's existence. Everything matters from ᒪᓂᑑ manitôw, cosmic creator, to ᒪᓂᒎᐢ manicôs, the little creator. Everyone is special, but we are not unique.

He alluded to it many times – ᐊ ᑳᔭ ᑯᓂᑕ a kâya konita, don't do it for nothing (don't do it for pity's sake).

I heard this decades ago. The reality of living in the moment and doing what you can with and in that moment – for me, it continues to be challenging and difficult. My trouble is, I spend time lamenting the past and worrying about the future. Living in the now brings to fore the mindset of ᐋᐧᓇᐦ wânah, peace and serenity. Belly laughs with family and friends and living with that joy help us stay in the moment, as does gratitude. There are so many other methods or activities that help keep us in the moment, like ceremony, cleaning (like cleaning medicines or your home), being on the land, ad infinitum ...

Bringing joviality to any moment of celebration, even Christmas, even Canada Day.

ᑮᐦᑌᐊᔭᐦ kîhtêayah, my late brother Emil used to say, where people are talking about God, ᐁᑯᑌ ᑐᐦᑌ êkote tohtê, go there and include yourself, count yourself, ᐊᑭᒥᓱᐦ akimisoh, and count yourself as one of them, count yourself as one of them, rather than separating yourself. Bring like ideas together.

This song helps us introduce ourselves to ᑮᓯᑳᐤ kîsikâw. The morning song, as people call it.

ᐊᐧᓂᐢᑳ
ᐊᐧᓂᐢᑳ ᐯᑕᐸᐣ ᐆᒪ
ᓵᓭᐩᐲᔦᓰᓵᐠ ᓂᑲᒨᐊᐧᐠ
ᐯᒦᔭᓈᑲᐧᐣ ᑭᑕᐢᑮᓇᐤ

waniskâ
waniskâ petapan ôma
sâsay pîyesîsâk nikamowak

pemiyonâkwan kitaskînaw

wake up! get up!
this dawn is coming
already the little birds they are singing
it comes looking good, our earth[18]

As ᐋᔩᓰᔩᓇᐤ âyîsîyînaw we are part of the spark of the supreme being. The world view is embedded in the language and ᐋ â permeates through the language, ᐊᔩᑭᐢ ayîkis, ᓵᑮᔩᑐᐠ sâkîyîtok, ᓵᑮᔩᑐᐏᐣ sâkîyitowin, love. ᐘᓂᐢᑳ waniskâ, the morning song, welcomes the day.

ᐘᓂᐢᑳ waniskâ, the morning song, and the ᑭᐢᑮᐍᐦᐅᐣ kiskîwêhon, the treaty flag song (that we talk about later), I know that these ones are shared openly. And anyone can sing them. Conversely, sacred songs are carefully looked after and not easily or readily shared.

What I would like you to do during the full moon is some good ᓀᐦᐄᔭᐤ nêhîyaw yoga. This comes from my granny. Though she didn't call it ᓀᐦᐄᔭᐤ nêhîyaw yoga! I did. So, get rid of all of your twenty-seven days of picking up all that negative energy stuff, and do the full moon exercise. Wonderful. So, it's real simple now. So, you're handing over something to someone now. And what is that something? And that's all of your things that are not beneficial for you, all those negative things. But there's also positive things that might not be beneficial for you. There's those things there. Some people like to say, you know, people with boundary issues. They're so nice, you know, that they let people walk all over them sometimes, those things, positive things

---

18 There are many versions of this song on *YouTube*, but listen to the version sung by the late Simon Kytwayhat from Loon Lake, Saskatchewan.

that are not beneficial. But what you're getting rid of is all of those things that are not beneficial for you. Doesn't matter what anybody else thinks, they're not good for you. You're going to get rid of them. You want to get rid of that, you know, or maybe being judgmental, whatever, all kinds of things, or else saying yes too much, you know, and maybe you're tired and somebody said, "hey, you want to do this?" and you don't want to let them down, you say yes. You know, maybe getting rid of that trait, you know, knowing when to take care of yourself and to look after your being.

"My sicknesses, my defects – here, take them."

(We're going to use this as a plural because it's plural here.)

"*Take them, my defects, my illnesses, my sicknesses.*"

ᓇᐦ ᐅᑎᓇᐦ ᓂᑕᐦ ᑯᓲᐏᓇᐦ

At each full moon, go outside, face the moon, brush yourself off from head to feet and then stand with your legs spread wide, your feet on the ground, raise your two arms towards the moon. Use your body, be coddled by the ethereal!

With your arms raised, say,
"ᓇᐦ ᐅᑎᓇᐦ ᓂᑕᐦᑯᓲᐏᓇᐦ
nah otinah nitahkosôwinah
Here, take all my sickness."

You are addressing the moon. You are asking the moon to take away your sickness, your frailties, your pain. She is big enough. She is big enough to take all of your ᐊᐦᑯᓲᐏᓇᐦ ahkosôwinah.

Enjoy earth's love. It is all around you.

The earth embraces us, loves us. She holds us.

ᑭᑳᐑᔨᓇᐤ ᐊᐢᑮᕀ kikâwîyinaw-askîy, our earth mother –

we are spinning and yet we do not fall off.

painting by Kaitlyn Purcell

The fourth law, make it strong, having discipline.

To overcome something – barriers, challenges – you need strength. It requires a lot of discipline. It requires a lot of strength. Try to learn discipline from an early age. So that we have some practical tools and practical application, and our language that will give us balance. Helps us to maintain balance. ᓲᐦᑲᐢᑣᐠ sôhkastwâk is hard to translate into English – strong, disciplined, focused.

ᓲᐦᑭᐦ sôhkih, hard, an effort, a hard effort. As if you are pushing a car out of a ditch. You need this law to work with the others.

ᓀᐦᐄᔭᐍᐏᐣ nêhîyawêwin is very practical.

Like the old ladies would tell us to tie our hair.

It was just after the nuns and priests left and some of us males had started growing our hair. It was mandatory prior, in the residential school era, that us Indian kids have short hair, brush cut. The old ladies said, "ᑮᐦᒉᔨᒥᓱᐠ kîhcêyimisok," respect yourselves, keep your dignity. Tie your hair to show that respect and dignity. They would say, "ᓲᐦᑲᐢᑣᐠ sôhkastwâk," be disciplined, stand strong.

The nuns had taught the residential school kids to hold back their tears. So, when we were in the schools we had to learn not to cry. There was loneliness, hardship. There were straps, and there were strict ways to deal with us. So, we learned to bring our tears back into our own bodies. The old ladies came when Blue Quills residential school was closed and taught the kids how to cry, again to let the tears come out. After the schools were closed, when the old ladies came, they explained how we were putting our tears into our own bodies. They told us that we needed to let our tears come out of our bodies out onto our faces. The old ladies drew a line with their finger from their eyes down their faces. They said when we do it the other way, keeping our tears in our body, we are poisoning ourselves. Science has proven this.

ᒫᑐᑎᓵᐣ mâtotisân is how you will hear the word today for sweat lodge. I have been taught that ᒫᑐᑎᓵᐣ mâtotisân is the old way to say "sweat lodge." Nowadays most people say "ᒪᑐᐟᓵᐣ matot'sân."

ᒫᑐᐦ mâto means "to cry." The ᒫᑐᑎᓵᐣ mâtotisân, sweat lodge, is a place for tears. There the four elements are used: fire, earth, water, air. These four sacred spirits, ᐃᐢᑯᑌᐤ iskotêw, ᐊᐢᑮᕀ askîy, ᓂᐲᕀ nipîy, ᔫᑎᐣ yôtin, are the ones that are called upon to hold the outcome of the people's prayers. In the lodge, the people sit on the earth. The ᐅᐢᑳᐯᐤ oskâpêw brings in hot rocks which have been heated in fire. They bring in water. And then they close the door of ᒫᑐᑎᓵᐣ mâtotisân, the sweat lodge, and the facilitator pours the water on the hot rocks, which creates steam. When they open the door, the first one to come into ᒫᑐᑎᓵᐣ mâtotisân, the lodge, is ᔫᑎᐣ yôtin with a breath of fresh air; the first one to leave the lodge is that steam, and it goes out like a teardrop. So, we go in there to release our troubles and give them to the sacred ones, the grandfathers and grandmothers, in the name of ᐋ â.

In the grandmother's lodge, everyone is special. This feels good there, I love it. The grandmother buffalo just welcomes everybody. And nobody is left out, even the one who's pouring the water. It's just as if we were all to go to our granny's home, all of us would be loved by our granny. No one is more exceptional.

Yes, I'm special, but I'm not unique. Everyone in that lodge is special. But not unique.

Yeah, it helps you live, it helps you move on.

And it's those elements, eh, that are included in there. There's fire, there's air, there's water, and there's earth. All the elements in there. And the four directions are in there. They are superimposed all over the place, reminding us, ᑲᑭᐢᑭᓰᔭᐦ kakiskisîyah.

And those elements don't have to have directions. Those ones, they're everywhere. They are another form of sacred spirit.

Respect the lodge you are visiting, following their rules and protocols, which might be different from what you are used to, or different from the way things are done elsewhere. This is ᓲᐦᑲᐢᑖᐏᐣ sôhkastwâwin, the fourth law. Each ceremony has its own protocols and standards. Each of us goes into ceremony with our own life and ceremony experiences. Your thoughts and feelings are challenged. You can experience cognitive, emotional, physical, and spiritual dissonance. However, being at ceremonies in the spirit of willingness and challenging the dissonance, we experience envelopment from the elements. We feel that we are home somehow. That we are where we should be. ᓲᐦᑲᐢᑖᐏᐣ sôhkastwâwin helps us to engage in difficult matters with faith.

These patterns, these ceremonies, people followed in their day-to-day lives, and for some people they still are, and for some people, these ways are growing again.

In our kinship systems, you didn't refer to each other by names but by connection. Indirect communication between close relations was important in the old days. You did not talk to your in-laws directly. To interact with the person that you encounter, proper names didn't work, you noted your relationship to them. Some people still use this system. I don't call my cross-cousin Eleanor by her name; her late dad and my late mom are brother and sister, and I call her nîtim.

And these familial structures are present in the larger schematic hierarchy from the old way of life. In practising, in using terminologies with relatives, it helps us to give the required humility needed to address each other and the sacred spirits. In example, I do not look at ᑭᒧᓲᒥᓇᐤ ᐲᓯᒼ kimosôminaw pîsim and say its name. I address that grandfather as ᓂᒧᓲᒼ nimosôm, my grandfather.

There was a governance system in old ᓀᐦᐃᔭᐘᐠ nêhîyawak society. It consisted of: ᐅᑮᐦᒌᐦᑖᐤ ᐃᐢᑫᐘᐠ okîhcîhtwâw iskwêwak, highly revered, highly respected females. I was told these ᐃᐢᑫᐘᐠ iskwêwak had jurisdiction over languages and medicines.

ᒥᑌᐤ mitêw, undisputed leader or prophet. I don't know much about ᒥᑌᐘᐠ mitêwak, only that they were gifted. My late uncle Jerry Quinn told me that our grandfather, ᐸᐦᐹᐢᑌᐤ pahpâstêw, is one of those.

ᐊᑯᐦᐱᔩᐑᔩᓇᐘᐠ akohpiyîwîyînawak – blanket people. I don't know anything about what the blanket people did.

ᑮᐦᒋᑮᐦᑌᐊᔭᐠ kîhcikîhte ayak – highly revered, highly respected elders

ᒪᐎᒨᐢᒋᑫᐑᔩᓂᐘᐠ mawimôscikewîyînawak – ceremony people

In ᓀᐦᐄᔭᐍᐏᐣ nêhîyawêwin, the gender is animate and inanimate, as was taught by Dr. Marilyn Shirt when I was teaching ᓀᐦᐄᔭᐍᐏᐣ nêhîyawêwin. We don't follow the gender in English ideology where there is male and female. In ᓀᐦᐄᔭᐍᐏᐣ nêhîyawêwin there was no gender that way, but when English came, we called everyone "him." So, it is hard to explain. I don't like to use the word "man." It seems aggressive to me – patriarchal. And "woman," from what I understand, is from "wife of man." She is basically property. So, it seems less offensive to use "female," and that is what I like to use.[19] So, what happens there when those two trains of thought come together? I don't know.

In ᓀᐦᐄᔭᐍᐏᐣ nêhîyawêwin, ᐃᐢᑵᐤ iskwêw, female, this is the one who determines future generations. ᑭᐢᑰᐘᐦᐃᑫᐤ kiskôwahikêw, a prophet, can prophesize the future, has the ability to foretell, to shape the future. Something like a forecaster: ᐅᑭᐢᑯᐍᐦᐃᑫᐤ okiskowêhikêw. The word for female, ᐃᐢᑵᐤ iskwêw, comes from this concept – from the verb ᑭᐢᑯᐍᐦ kiskowêh, prophesy. ᐄᑭᐢᑰᐍᐦᔩᑫᐟ îkiskôwêyîkêt, she is prophesying. Females have the bodily capability of bringing future life and therefore, literally, prophesize the future. This is one interpretation of where this word, ᐃᐢᑵᐤ iskwêw, comes from. One year, I took my class to a ceremony, ᐄᓂᐹᑵᐦᐋᐦᑭᐠ înipâkwêhâhkik, a sundance singing at Saddle Lake, and we learned this teaching from Noah Cardinal. There are other interpretations.

One that I have heard is the connection to fire, ᐃᐢᑯᑌᐤ iskotêw. Saysewahum Sylvia McAdam mentions this.[20] What I want to

19 We checked the etymology of the word "female" and found that it is not linked to the etymology of the word "male."

20 Sylvia McAdam (Saysewahum), *Nationhood Interrupted: Revitalizing nêhiyaw Legal Systems* (UBC Press, 2015).

say is, howsoever we come to the interpretation of ᐃᐢᑫᐤ iskwêw, iskwêwak are the keystone to our future. The first ones that were attacked by colonization, you know, was those females there.

I use the word "female," like I said, because that's the closest I can get to ᐃᐢᑫᐤ iskwêw. Because they weren't property. I don't know how to explain it. It's just such a different system as I understand it.

Just such a different world view. Different world view. Different homes. Like I said, ᒦᑰᐚᐦᑊ mîkôwâhp or teepee teachings hold this integrated view.[21] According to these teachings, the teepee is a being, the fire inside is sacred. Back in the days when the ᓀᐦᐄᔭᐘᐠ nêhîyawak had their homes. There were the poles. The teepee poles were kept intact so that they'd have a function. Each pole had a law or a value attached to it, maybe not a law but a value attached to it. And ᐋᐸᓷᐚᓈᐦᑎᑿᐦ âpasôwânâhtikwah, the poles, were portable. They were disassembled and transported from site to site. And the stitch pegs on the teepee – from top to bottom. So, you know, they had their functions, too. The flaps had their functions. So, the home was an entity, a living being. From the fire, that hearth, the fire within was sacred. Now where do most of us get our fire from? From the stove? Now we make it a commodity. We've forgotten the sacredness of fire. Its spirit. We made the earth a commodity in our mindset. The animals, they are a commodity. They're ours. It's not like we all belong to the earth. Now humans are at the top of the food chain. They talk about the food chain. All humans are at the top of the food chain. And there's a hierarchy to the body, too. The settlers developed their language to serve their world view, and that has been adopted by many of us now.

21 The Lakota word ᒦᑰᐚᐦᑊ mîkôwâhp, teepee, has become the word appropriated by English.

Using a ᓀᐦᐃᔭᐤ nêhîyaw world view, I have learned that the profane is also sacred. For instance, ᐯᑭᑐᐦ pwêkitoh, passing gas, farting, is considered rude nowadays. In ᓀᐦᐃᔭᐍᐏᐣ nêhîyawêwin there is a sacred name for ᐯᑭᑐᐦ pwêkitoh, who is ᒣᒧᐦᒑᕽ mêmohcâhk (the ᒑᕽ câhk makes it spirit). Where I have heard this word is in the ᓂᐹᑵᓯᒨᐃᐧᑲᒥᑿᐦ nipâkwêsimôwikamikwah, the sundances, and ᒫᑐᑎᓵᓇᐦ mâtotisânah, sweat lodges. Lots of pressure happens in those ᒫᑐᑎᓵᓇᐦ mâtotisânah sweat lodges! As with everyone else, ᒣᒧᐦᒑᕽ mêmohcâhk was conceived by ᒪᓂᑑᐤ manitôw, creator, or someone who creates.

ᒪᓂᑑᐑᐦᑕᑖᐟ manitôwîhtatât – someone who is creating.

For instance, what the sun does is ᐄ ᒪᓂᑑᐑᐦᑕᑖᐟ î manitôwîhtatât – he is creating, like photosynthesis.

What the earth does is ᒪᓂᑑᐑᐦᑕᑖᐟ manitôwîhtatât.
ᐄᒪᓂᑑᐑᐦᑕᑖᐟᐅᑳᐢᑭᑲᐣ î manitôwîhtatât okâskikan
She creates with her chest, with her body, our mother the earth, with her chest, her body, her torso, she creates with this.

Who else creates? Who else does that? ᓂᐲᕀ nipîy. Where does water come from?
ᐲᔦᓲᐤ ᐄᓈᑲᑌᔩᐦᑕᐦ pîyesôw înâkatêyîhtah – the thunderbird looks after the water.
ᐄᒪᓂᑑᐑᐦᑕᑖᐟ ᓂᐲᕀ î manitôwîhtatât nipîy

What do they do, these ones?
ᐲᔦᓲᐤ pîyesôw looks after the water.
ᐲᔦᓲᐤ ᐄᓈᑲᑌᔩᐦᑕᐦ pîyesôw înâkatêyîhtah

However, ᐲᔦᓲᐤ pîyesôw also infuses the water with its power.
ᐄᒪᓂᑑᐑᐦᑕᑖᐟ ᓂᐲᕀ î manitôwîhtatât nipîy

ᐋᔦᓲᐤ pîyesôw is infusing power into that which they are looking after.
That is what ᐄᒪᓂᑑᐄᐦᑕᑖᐟ î manitôwîhtatât means.

ᔫᑎᐣ ᐄᒪᓂᑑᐄᐦᑕᑖᐟ ᑳ ᔦᐦᐁᑐᑕᒪᕽ
yôtin î manitôwîhtatât kâ yêhêtotamahk
ᔫᑎᐣ yôtin, it looks after that which we breathe. It infuses that which we breathe with its power. In essence it continually gives us ᐱᒫᑎᓲᐏᐣ ᑭᒦᔨᑯᓇᐤ pimâtisôwin kimîyikonaw, life.
He gives us life.

This is true for all of them:
ᐃᐢᑯᑌᐤ iskotêw, fire, ᐊᐢᑮᕀ askîy, earth, ᓂᐲᕀ nipîy, water, ᔫᑎᐣ yôtin, wind.
ᐃᐢᑵᐤ ᐄ ᒪᓂᑑᐄᐦᑕᑖᐟ ᐱᒫᑎᓲᐏᐣ iskwêw î manitôwîhtatât pimâtisôwin.

The elements have their own laws.
Humans, we have our own laws.
Females can create. They make us. They make life.

Essentially, there are many creators, and there is one that binds us all together and that one is ᐋ â. ᐋ â is the one that gives ᒪᓂᑑᐤ manitôw powers. Those spirits were given that to do. They were given those powers. Some people are given other ᒪᓂᑑᐤ manitôw powers as well.

Ultimately, when you say "my creator," you are addressing ᐋ, ᑮᐦᒋᒪᓂᑑᐤ kîhcimanitôw or ᐋ, ᑭᓭᒪᓂᑑ kisêmanitôw. Whether you put ᑮᐦᒋ kîhci or ᑭᓭ kisê, when you say "ᐋ," you are addressing the greatest higher power. ᐋ is the ultimate creator. ᐋ is who we are referring to when we say "ᑮᐦᒋᒪᓂᑑᐤ kîhcimanitôw."[22]

22 When you say ᐋ, ᑮᐦᒋᒪᓂᑑᐤ â, kîhcimanitôw, you are describing

ᒪᓂᒎᐢ manicôs, translated into English as "insect" or "bug," they are a diminutive of ᒪᓂᑑᐤ manitôw. Therefore, ᒪᓂᒎᐢ manicôs, it is little creator because they are life.[23] The English translation loses this understanding.

If we stop listening, if we stop listening or we stop hearing. And yeah, I was thinking about that. Like the way the water can speak to us or the way the earth is always speaking to us. It has to be. When I don't listen. If I don't want to, I lose the ability to connect. Now, I'm talking in general as a human species. There are so many distractions – like phones, like TV. We lose the ability to connect, and we separate ourselves from the natural world. We separate ourselves and develop a language to serve our view, our world view. That's what we've done.

ᓀᐦᐄᔭᐍᐏᐣ nêhîyawêwin reminds us of ᐚᐦᑯᐦᑑᐏᐣ wâhkohtôwin. ᓀᐦᐄᔭᐤ nêhîyaw culture reminds us two-legged people to observe protocol, to listen. In so doing we have honour and respect for all of our relatives in the other five nations.

A common protocol I would like to share now is for greeting friends. I also greet ᑮᓯᑳᐤ kîsikâw, day, and ᒦᑐᓴᐠ mîtosak, trees, and other relatives in this way:

---

who ᐋ â is; that is, ᑮᐦᒋᒪᓂᑑᐤ kîhcimanitôw. ᑮᐦᒋᐦ kîhcih means the most highly revered and highly respected ᒪᓂᑑᐤ manitôw, and ᒪᓂᑑᐤ manitôw means creator. You say this when you are going into prayer and you are addressing the creator.

ᑭᓭ kisê means ultimate kindness. ᑭᓭᒪᓂᑑᐤ kisêmanitôw is the kindest creator, and you would say this in prayer, asking for that ultimate kindness to go towards someone.

ᐲᓯᒼ pîsim is also ᒪᓂᑑᐤ manitôw, so is ᔫᑎᐣ yôtin and ᐲᔦᓲᐤ piyesôw. On a smaller level, the insect is also called ᒪᓂᒎᐢ manicôs (little creator). They are all creators and for us, ᐋ â is the kindest, the most compassionate creator of all. That is ᑭᓭᒪᓂᑑᐤ kisêmanitôw.

23 This teaching comes from Neil Red Crow.

ᐋ â, I acknowledge your being
ᓂᐅᑑᑌᒥᑎᐠ niotôtêmitik, my friends
ᑭᐊᑕᒥᐢᑳᑎᓈᐚᐤ ki atamiskâtinâwâw, I greet you
ᑲᐦᑮᔭᐤ kahkîyaw, all

ᐊᐦᐋᐤ ᓂᐅᑑᑌᒥᑎᐠ ᑭᐊᑕᒥᐢᑳᑎᓈᐚᐤ ᑲᐦᑮᔭᐤ
ahâw niotôtêmitik ki atamiskâtinâwâw kahkîyaw
â, I acknowledge your being, my friends, I greet you all

_______ᓂᑎᓰᐦᑲᓱᐣ nitisihkâson, my name is __________.

_______ᐅᐦᒋᓃᔭᐦ ohcinîyah, I am from ___________.

There are also protocols for gathering berries or stones or anything.

Find out from the people from the land you are on how you might harvest something.

Gathering protocol – introduce yourself, acknowledge the creator:

ᐋ â behold
acknowledge the earth, our mother.
nikâwîy, my mother.
and you acknowledge the relative that you are picking, berry or plant.
ᓂᐘᐦᑰᒪᑲᐣ niwahkômâkan, my relative,
ᑭᐊᑕᒥᐢᑳᑎᐣ kiatamiskâtin, I greet you!
ᐋ ᓂᐘᐦᑰᒪᑲᐣ ᑭᐊᑕᒥᐢᑳᑎᐣ
â niwahkômâkan kiatamiskâtin
behold my relative, I greet you!

Acknowledge to that being that you gather, say your prayer, ask for help, give the being (that rock, those berries, those grasses) thanks for blessing you. Lay your tobacco down (enough to fill a pipe or make a cigarette) and ask that relative to help and come home with you.

As an example, when I pick ᓃᐱᓰᓴᐠ nîpisîsak, willows, I am reminded always who I am going to for help. I understand, from what I have been told, in this case, that I am basically destroying a whole ecosystem. Micro-organisms, insects, birds, four-leggeds depend on this ᓃᐱᓰᐢ nîpisîs, willow relative. So, when I am thinking about harvesting, I have to remember the life of the ᓃᐱᓰᐢ nîpisîs I am taking. But also, the effect it will have on that system. The ᓃᐱᓰᐢ nîpisîs makes a great sacrifice. That is all I want to say about that for now.

After the first thunder, that's when you got permission to go picking, too. After the first thunder, you can go and pick medicines. That's a law, that's a treaty. Otherwise, if you go pick a medicine, between fall and spring, you have to follow different protocol. It's like you're approaching another human being, and that human being's got something for you. And it's important. It's life, life or death. So, you offer that person protocol. And maybe even ᐅᐢᐿᑲᐣ ospwâkan, a pipe. So, you would do that in a winter, in a fall or in a winter. If you needed a medicine for life or death, you would have a ceremony and call upon that plant that you want. And then you would go after that, you would go and dig that plant out or take the stem off or take a bark off or something. So, you would follow protocol. That's about that respect, love, honour, trust, and respect between nations. And that's the six nations. So, one of the six nations is the plant nation. So, those people too, they accept protocol. And that's how we receive their grace. That's how they save our dignity, our lives, too. If we respect those protocols. That's how they save our dignity. Yeah, we think that we're saving our own dignity when we're offering protocol. But they have life. They have ᐱᒼ pim.

ᐱᒼ pim is from the chart, the south grandfather direction, from ᐱ. And ᐱ holds the thirteenth law – ᑭᔮᒪᐱᐦ kiyâmapih, to let go.

I am mostly talking here about the first four laws, but you need the first law with all of them. To stand strong and with a good effort with the first law ᓵᑮᔩᑐᐠ sâkîyîtok, you need to know what love is. Not society's idea, which, to me, is kind of skewed. Love is exuding positive vibes, blossoming, emanating positive vibes, and standing strong in there, trying not to go overboard. To stand strong in the second law. To help each other ᐐᒌᔨᑐᐠ wîcîyitok, that which is helpful for the people, not for individual gains. The whole of the people – to help the whole of the people. You stay disciplined. You are there to help and you need to accept help. For that one you also really need that third law – ᒦᔪᐚᑕᒧᐠ mîyowâtamok, to enjoy life. And for that one you also need the fourth law so that you don't go too far, don't have too much fun. So, we have to be disciplined, ᓲᐦᑲᐢᏔᐧᐠ sôhkastwâk, and we need to teach the little ones discipline, too. During raids the moms would hold their hands over the baby's mouths so that they wouldn't cry when enemies were coming. In those days discipline was a matter of life or death. It still can be.

There were and are many other ways, too, of learning discipline: discipline in ceremony, discipline in social situations, discipline in economics, familial discipline, and in natural law, too.

Part of understanding natural law comes from addressing the creative intelligence, understanding the universal being as one organism. Our numbered treaties are based on this understanding. The earliest treaties that existed between the humans and the elements – ᐲᓯᒼ pîsim, ᐊᐢᑮᕀ askîy, ᓂᐲᕀ nipîy,

ᔫᑎᐢ yôtin, as long as the sun shines, the grass grows, the waters flow, and the four winds blow. No one mentions the wind any more these days, but I got that word of mouth back in the seventies. As long as the green grass grows, the sun shines, the water flows, and the four winds blow. The treaty includes all the elements, and in the old days all ᓀᐦᐄᔭᐤ nêhîyaw people follow god's law – the sun rises in the east, sets in the west. In every spring season, the grasses begin to grow, and the waters begin to flow. The four winds continually blow. The birds return as they always have, and those who hibernate come out as well. In the autumn, the geese fly south, and the bear will hibernate or fast. This is natural law, and ᐲᓯᒼ pîsim, ᐊᐢᑮᕀ askîy, ᓂᐲᕀ nipîy, ᔫᑎᐣ yôtin were all included in the treaties.

In ᓀᐦᐄᔭᐍᐏᐣ nêhîyawêwin, ᐊᓱᒋᑫᐏᐣ asocikêwin is a treaty. For the ᐄᔩᓇᐤ îyînaw nations, treaty is like ᐋᓱᑲᐣ âsokan, a bridge.
ᐊᓱᒋᑫᐏᐣ asocikêwin – treaty/promise
ᐋᓱᐦ âsoh – passing something on in continuation, one to another
ᐋᓱᑲᐣ âsokan – bridge
ᐊᓱᑕᒫᐏᐣ asotamâwin – promise

ᐊᓱᒋᑫᐏᐣ asocikêwin is connected to the word for promise. I used to hear the old people use this word. The promise is ᐊᓱᑕᒪᐍᐤ asotamawêw, she/he or it (animate) promise(s) something. To make a promise is to make a bridge, to go across – nation to nation. And the elements were used, like ᐃᐢᑯᑌᐤ iskotew, fire. Those beings were the mnemonic system used to remind us of the bridging between the nations (they continue to remind us). The elements are also treaty partners and witnesses to the promises. The treaty, the bridge, the promises are alive as long as the elements exist and they cannot not exist: ᐃᐢᑯᑌᐤ iskotêw, fire, ᐊᐢᑮᕀ askîy, earth, ᓂᐲᕀ nipîy, water, ᔫᑎᐣ yôtin, the wind.

ᐋᓱᑲᐣ âsokan is a transference. A bridge transfers something. The treaty acts as a bridge. It bridges; it is a crossing over.

It is ᐚᐦᑯᐦᐦᑑᐃᐧᐣ wâhkohtôwin, relationship building.

ᐊᓱᑕᒫᐃᐧᐣ asotamôwin, it's the word that means "promise(s)." And one of the things that we're always cautioned is not to make promises. We're told, especially with children, that if you promise a child something, a youngster, and you break that promise, in our world view, that's a real bad decision. It's not good for anyone when you break a promise to a child. There is always a witness. The four elements bear witness. Whether it is the air or the land we stand on, there is always a witness. So, we're always told – ᑳᔭᐦ ᐊᓱᒋᑫ kâyah asocikê.

Which means "don't make promises." An unfulfilled or broken promise leads to ᐹᐢᑖᐦᐆᐃᐧᐣ pâstâhôwin. Which, to me, means shattering the future.

And so, when treaties were being made, the British North America Act. Did we come across that already? The British North America Act actually was very, very instrumental in enforcing genocide. And so, the treaties were seen by the ᓀᐦᐄᔭᐘᐠ nêhîyawak as a place where there could be an opportunity, a chance for ... for the race to go on. So, there they made promises not to fight anymore. The idea was that we could make a livelihood using European methods, because the entire food source, almost the entire food source of the ᐄᔩᓇᐤ îyînaw was killed off by then. They say it was tens of millions of buffalo. There's some people say 100 million buffalo. I don't know the number, but by 1885, from what I was told, there were only five hundred head of ᒧᐢᑐᓴᐠ mostosak, buffalo, left, and that was in the middle of Montana. There were invasive species introduced as well, and the prairie ecosystem was changed. Many food sources had almost been completely wiped out, which weakened the position of the ᐄᔩᓇᐤ îyînaw people at the bargaining table because of hunger, because of famine. There were 100 million ᐄᔩᓇᐤ îyînaw people here on turtle island. Today, in Canada, there are 1.8 million ᐄᔩᓇᐤ îyînaw people who identify as indigenous, according to the 2021 census.

So, these people, ᑭᒥᐢᑕᒣᒫᑲᓂᓇᐘᐠ kimistamêmâkaninawak, our ancestors, there thought, "well, we have to think about our children, and we have to think about their livelihood. The buffalo are gone, and there's this new way, this farming way, and there's a way of understanding that system." And education was one of the things that treaty 6 covered with education and health care, and that health care had to do with being able to deal with the new diseases that were coming up. And so, they, the ᓀᐦᐃᔭᐤ nêhîyaw, decided to go this route, to make that treaty with the British. So they said, now, these promises will be kept as long as the sun shines, the grass grows, the rivers flow, and the four winds blow. That's what I was told by people. My dad and my uncle told me that. And it was my dad's grandfather, ᐸᐦᐹᐢᑌᐤ pahpâstêw, who signed the adhesion to treaty 6. So, these promises go on for as long as those times are available – ᐊᓱᑕᒫᐃᐧᓇᐦ asotamâwinah, promises. I like that word, yeah. Here in Edmonton, there is a river that goes through the city, and there's places where they made ᐋᓱᑲᓇᐦ âsokanah, these bridges. And those ᐋᓱᑲᓇᐦ âsokanah are awesome and allow you to go from one shore to another. It helps you cross them so you can see us again and again.

In this case, these ᐊᓱᑕᒫᐃᐧᓇᐦ asotamâwinah become promises and this ᐋᓱᑲᐣ âsokan becomes a bridge. Just a little something to think about as far as language and vernacular is concerned.

So, they did this, ᓀᐦᐃᔭᐘᕽ nêhîyawak made promises with the ᐅᐢᐹᑲᐣ ospwâkan pipe, ᒪᐢᑯᓰᔫᐏᐦᑲᐢᑿᐦ maskosîyôwîhkaskwah, sweetgrasses and ᒋᐢᑌᒫᐤ cistêmâw, tobacco.

In the treaty-making process, ᐅᐢᐹᑲᐣ ospwâkan, the pipe, was present. It was also a witness and insured the truth of the promises made.

ᐅᐢᐹᑲᐣ ospwâkan, the pipe, is very important as well in the ethereal. Because it's one of the seven sacred spirits that sits directly with ᐋ, the creator. So, the number seven again becomes symbolic and significant. There can be no lies when ᐅᐢᐹᑲᐣ ospwâkan, the pipe, is joined, stem and stone, only ᑖᐴᐍᐏᐣ tâpôwêwin, truth.

ᐅᐢᐹᑲᐣ ospwâkan, the pipe, has been part of our ceremony life, forever.

Back in the day, I was told by my brother, Clifford Cardinal, when they were making the pipe stem, they would find a termite first and then get a berry-bearing stem. A fire would be made. They would take that stem and put it on the ground and cover the stem and termite together. Then, they would get a coal and put it behind the termite. You'd have to be so careful not to hurt that termite. The termite would have no choice but to eat its way through the cork of the berry-bearing stem, which is the softest part. This is how the pipe stem was made. So, the pipe – the stone and the stem were put together that way. That was how people would do it. Because they didn't have wires, of course, back then.

One of the old people said that, you know, in that pipe, with that pipe, smoked during the treaty talks, the ᓀᐦᐃᔭᐤ nêhîyaw promised to look after the Europeans, no matter what. So, what does that mean? Well, it means that whatever we have, we have to learn how to share it. Like if we have something spiritual, but some things need to be learned and there has to be protocol. Like ᒫᑐᑎᓵᐣ mâtotisân, the sweat lodge. I fasted for that. And some people are coming out and talking about those things. That's what I like. Like Jimmy O'Chiese. You know, Jimmy O'Chiese, his people, from around Hinton, they did not take treaty. And he said, "your cousins," "your cousins," not "our cousins." He said, to us, that took treaty, "your cousins, you need to look after them!" Meaning, you, who signed treaty, promised to take care of the people who came and were to come. And when the wind blows through the flag (back then the Union Jack and now the Canadian flag) we are reminded of the responsibilities and obligations entered into at the time of treaty making – ᑭᐢᑮᐍᐦᐅᐣ kiskîwêhon, flag.

In 1876 when treaty 6 was signed by first nations and the Crown, each chief who signed the treaty was given, among other items, a Union Jack flag and a treaty 6 medal to honour the treaties, honoured by all people, those waters, the air, the grass, the earth, the blood of our mother – words that people can hang on to, to blow life into.

To honour treaty 6, this song was composed by humans in the early 1900s.[24]

ᑭᐦᒌᑭᒫᐢᑫᐤ kihcôkimâskwêw
ᑭᑮᒦᔩᑯᓇᐤ kikîmîyikonaw
ᑭᐢᑮᐍᐦᐅᐣ kiskîwêhon
ᑳᑭᑫ ᑲᐑᐁᐹᐢᑕᐣ kâkikê ka wî wepâstan

24 According to Arden Ogg, citing E. J. Tootoosis Sr., "the rights to sing this was granted by the kayasiwatom family to the Tootoosis singers." Arden Ogg, "Tyrone Tootoosis, Sr. on the Treaty Six Flag," *Cree Literacy Network*, September 12, 2013, creeliteracy.org/2013/09/12/tyrone-tootoosis-sr-on-the-treaty-six-flag/.

The queen
gave unto us
the flag
may it forever wave in the wind.[25]
The literal translation is this:

The big boss Woman,
she had given us the flag
forever it will move from side to side.

ᑭᐢᑮᐍᐦᐅᐣ kiskîwêhon, ᑭᐢᑭᐦ kiskih, the flag, it helps you remember.

ᑭᐢᑮᐍᐦᐅᐣ kiskîwêhon, that flag holds their prayers for themselves and for seven generations forward. ᑳᑮᔨᓯᒨᐏᐣ kâkîyisimôwin, prayer, was paramount at those treaty talks. At this time there was famine. So, what did they do? The old people were starving to death because they saved the food for the children. The leaders discussed and decided treaty with the British was the only option. They came together, and with all the powers that they were given and that they had, they used ᑳᑮᔨᓯᒨᐏᐣ kâkîyisimôwin. Some were ᒥᑌᐘᐠ mitêwak, powerful leaders. They came together to stop genocide.

So, what happened then, at the treaty talks, the pipe was smoked. All the ᓀᐦᐃᔭᐘᐠ nêhîyawak that were gathered there, they put their ᑳᑮᔨᓯᒨᐏᓇᐦ kâkîyisimôwinah on those flags, those prints.

---

25 This first translation is cited by Arden Ogg, "Northern Cree Flag Song – A Treaty Reminder," *Cree Literacy Network*, May 23, 2022, creeliteracy.org/2022/05/23/northern-cree-flag-song-a-treaty-reminder/. She notes her slight adjustments and attributes @TheCreebecois for their translation in the comments at "Northern Cree Flag Song," posted August 4, 2010, by shakeyoufast, *YouTube*, 4 min., 53 sec., www.youtube.com/watch?v=tSTVXaINRTs. You can hear Northern Crees' beautiful version of the treaty 6 song at this link.

So that the future of the ᓀᐦᐃᔭᐊᐧᐠ nêhîyawak would live on, would move on.

ᐍᐱᓈᓱᐣ wêpinâson, broadcloth, print, flag. So you put your words, your prayers, your positive vibes and love on ᐍᐱᓈᓱᐣ wêpinâson. The next step is to hang the ᐍᐱᓈᓱᐣ wêpinâson on a tree. Then the prayers, that were put on the ᐍᐱᓈᓱᐣ wêpinâson, they circle the earth forever. They are animate beings.

ᐅᑮᓯᑰᐊᐧᐠ okîsikôwak, specifically ᐃᐢᑯᑌᐤ iskotêw, ᐊᐢᑭᐩ askîy, ᓂᐲᐩ nipîy, and ᔫᑎᐣ yôtin, but not exclusively, are witness to those ᑳᑮᔨᓯᒨᐃᐧᓇᐦ kâkîyisimôwinah, and forever they remember.

ᑫᔮᐱᐨ ᐚᐦᐍᐹᐢᑕᐣ ᑭᐢᑮᐍᐦᐅᐣ
kêyâpic wâhwêpâstan kiskîwêhon
The flag still waves in the wind, the wind still moves in the flag.

And with ᐅᐢᐚᑲᐣ the ospwâkan, the pipe, there can be no lies. With the pipe put together, there can be no lies.

ᐋᓂᐢᑯᑖᐯ aniskotâpe, you make the link. The context is that with ᐅᐢᐚᑲᐣ ospwâkan, the pipe, there can be no lies, so you make the link by fitting ᐅᐢᑭᒌᐩ oskicîy, the pipe stem, into the ᐊᓯᓃᐩ asinîy, the stone bowl of the pipe, and with that the promises – those promises that were made there, the elements remind us of them. They didn't just stay there static. Because of the elements, those promises are always present. The elements, outside, ᔫᑎᐣ yôtin, the wind is still blowing and ᒪᐢᑯᓰᔭᐦ maskosîyah, the grasses are still growing, and they manifest those promises. As long as ᐲᓯᒼ pîsim, the sun, shines, ᒪᐢᑯᓰᔭᐦ maskosîyah, the green grasses, grow, ᓂᐲᐩ nipîy, the water, flows, and ᔫᑎᐣ yôtin, the four winds, blow. ᐅᐢᐚᑲᐣ ospwâkan, the pipe, was used at treaty talks between ᓀᐦᐃᔮᐤ nêhîyaw and the British.

The treaty laws are earth laws. The sun rises in the east and sets in the west. The treaty laws are god's law.

And yet, the British, they broke treaty time and again.

We are looking at the legal system in a different way. It is a different world view. The world view is classically different. I find that in Western thinking, everything is compartmentalized. Even sectors of your brain become so many compartments there. I think where that all started was with the advent of the agrarian societies. In Europe, they had agrarian societies. Yet, ᐄᔩᓇᐤ îyînaw nations were also agrarian. There were agrarian ways of life here, too, but what they didn't do was own the land. Those ᐄᔩᓇᐤ îyînaw nations looked at the land as we belong to the land, the land doesn't belong to us. And so, they have to take care of it that way.

Like turtle island, for instance, they would do control burning all the time to encourage the plant people to come back, and there's nitrogen going back to the earth, you know.

Nowadays most of us look at things from a scientific perspective. When you have that type of world view and you have owning rather than being. You say, "well, what is in the fire?" Well, nitrogen.

Same thing that's in a thunderbolt from ᐲᔦᓲᐤ pîyesôw. See, we have a relationship with that fire. And that fire cleanses the land. And it also encourages the vegetation to come back the following year. And that's what kept the buffalo, all those 100 million buffalo, alive.

Most of the ᓀᐦᐃᔭᐘᐠ nêhîyawak people were seminomadic here. They weren't nomadic. They were seminomadic. They moved camps from place to place, too, depending on what season it was. In the winter they had winter camps and in the summer, summer camps.

ᓀᐦᐄᔭᐘᐠ nêhîyawak have their teachings about laws, you know, treaties that we have and how to recognize those laws. Like, I think I told you already, the real simple laws, the law of ᐚ. Did I tell you that one? Well, the sun rises in the east and sets in the west. That's the law of ᐋ. Know that the birds will leave in the fall and come back in the spring. That's the law of ᐋ. So, we begin to look at the justice system, the legal system in a different way. What we do when we try to go against the law of ᐋ. Things happen to us like what we're doing to the land right now when we break treaty law. It goes against the law of ᐋ. To the extent that we're doing it. And, like, there's so many invasive species now – 80 percent of it is invasive species now.

ᐄ ᐊᐢᐳᓈᑎᓯᒋᐠ î asponâtisicik, and that means that they have it all, but they want some more. This explains why the treaties are eroded and attacked to keep ᐄᔩᓇᐤ îyînaw people down. There's different ways that the treaties are still being attacked and eroded by the government, you know, to keep ᐄᔩᓇᐤ îyînaw people down. The Canadian system is modelled after the European system, and its model is ownership, disconnected, unlistening, separation.

Well, we're linked with our dna. This whole earth. Our dna, we are all related. And that work, that work we need to do, you know, following the laws of ᐋ.

During the time of the treaties, there was still some fear on the part of the colonizers. The British, they told their people, "there's land out there." The settlers, they just had to work it, and it's free. As I understand it, they were assured by the Crown that the land was free because there were only "savages" there. In the British model, "savages" had no right to land ownership. In the British model, there were different values placed on the two-leggeds. Some humans were more valuable than others. This was true in the other colonial systems too: Spanish, Dutch, Portuguese, French.

So, at treaty time, the settlers wanted assurances. They agreed to come out here to farm the land. But at around the time of treaty 6, there was a lot of resistance in Manitoba. Louis Riel, Gabriel Dumont, and others fought a war against the illegal colonial occupation of the west.

So, the settlers wanted assurances that they would be protected, and the Crown agreed to make treaty as a result.

My late uncle, Jerry Quinn, and my late dad were visiting and talking about our late grandfather, ᐸᐦᐹᐢᑌᐤ pahpâstêw. ᐸᐦᐹᐢᑌᐤ pahpâstêw was trying to mount forces against the occupation. He sent ᒋᐢᑌᒫᐤ cistêmâw, tobacco, to other turtle island nations – that didn't go well, and things were bad in Saskatchewan, in Batoche. So, he had to take treaty, either be starved out or take treaty.

He put his mark there, on the treaty document. He put the ᕽ locative – the small spirit marker, "hk" in SRO. A locative is a linguistic term for a word that notes a location. An example I can use is the location of where I come from. ᐅᓃᐦᒋᑭᐢᑲᐘᐯᐏᓃᕽ onîhcikiskwapêwinîhk, Saddle Lake. The ᕽ, hk, at the end of the word means that the word is a place.

In the case of ᐸᐦᐹᐢᑌᐤ pahpâstêw, signing the treaty with the ᕽ, the small spirit marker, the locative – it marks a "hereness." It says, "I am here."

My brother, Carl, came into our class and gave a presentation on ᓀᐦᐄᔭᐍᐑᐣ nêhîyawêwin, ᐊᑖᐦᑭᐯᔩᐦᑲᓇᐠ atâhkipêyîhkanak, and ᐊᒑᐦᑭᐯᔩᐦᑲᓂᓴᐠ acâhkipêyîhkanisak. He spoke about each spirit marker and the work it does, and he talked about the locative ˣ and how ᐸᐦᐹᐢᑌᐤ pahpâstêw had put that mark, that ˣ, on the treaty document.

So, I want you to think about this paradigm difference. This difference in world views. We belong to the land. The land does not belong to us. That is what the locative says, wherever we go, there we are.

ᐊᓱᒋᑫᐦᒌᐦᑕᒨᐑᓂˣ – that means here, asocikehcîhtamôwinihk, where the promises are, here, in this place, in the elements – where the sun shines, the green grass grows, the river flows, and the four winds blow. Context is so important.

ᐁᑯᓯ ᑮ ᐃᑘᐘᐠ êkosi kî itwêwak – they said that.

This is what they had said, to reiterate the promises, to remind people for all time.

ᐁᑯᓯ ᑮ ᐃᑘᐘᐠ êkosi kî itwêwak: this is what they said, this is what they communicated, this is what was communicated. The morpheme indicates past tense, ᑮ kî. That is what they said and that is what they said, ˣ, here.

But what we were left with was the leftovers, ᐃᐢᑯᓂᑲᐣ iskonikan. How you might hear that these days is without the third spirit marker ᐃᐢᑯᐣᑲᐣ iskon'kan. These days, ᐃᐢᑯᐣᑲᐣ iskon'kan also means "reservation." They have everything, but they want more ᐄᐊᐢᐳᓈᑎᓯᒋᐠ î asponâtisicik (ᐄᐊᐢᐳᓈᑎᓯᐟ, î asponâtisit is singular) – the British, the settlers, they have it all, but they want more. So, when they, ᓀᐦᐄᔭᐘᐠ the nêhîyawak, signed treaty, they kept on seeing what was happening to the land. It was being gobbled up. We were left the scraps.

Why are we here talking about this? I hope something does come of us talking like this. Did the Queen ever come herself to turtle island to make treaty? No. Why not? Treaties were supposed to be made leader-to-leader. Instead, she sent her representatives.

The treaties were sacred agreements. They were laws: intellectual, material or practical, and spiritual laws, and they were broken.

After a time, the reserve ᐸᐦᐹᐢᑌᐤ pahpâstêw was promised and assigned through treaty became too valuable to the citizens of Fort Edmonton. They wanted that land for themselves. So, what happened after that, starvation and propaganda,[26] forced my grandfather ᐸᐦᐹᐢᑌᐤ pahpâstêw to take scrip, and the brothers went their separate ways. ᐸᐦᐹᐢᑌᐤ pahpâstêw went to St-Paul-de-Métis.

When the treaty was broken, this was ᐹᐢᑖᒨᐏᐣ pâstâmôwin. To me, pâstâmôwin means "to shatter someone's future." ᐹᐢᑖᐦᐆᐏᐣ pâstâhôwin means, to me, "to shatter the future." My father said that if we hadn't signed treaty, ᐄᔩᓇᐤ îyînaw genocide would have been complete. With the treaty promises, some received farm implements, cattle, horses. But not everyone. There were laws on this land and the British came over with their laws, but they primarily looked after property and individual rights. Yeah. Whereas, according to the ᐄᔩᓇᐤ îyînaw laws here, the individual is important, you know, special, but not unique. No one's unique. We're all special. Just not unique. Yeah. So, the whole is important – like a beehive. It was

26 Frank Oliver's newspaper used to vilify the people.

always looked at like that. In ᓀᐦᐄᔭᐤ nêhîyaw law, everyone is special, but no one is unique – the four-legged, the winged one, the water ones, the water itself. Everyone matters.

You know, even to hunt animals, there were laws. It was against the law to kill a ᑳᑿᐦ kâkwah, porcupine. There was no honour in killing a ᑳᑿᐦ kâkwah. Unless for ceremony or unless you were starving. They are a slow lumbering creature. ᒧᐢᑐᐢ mostos, the buffalo, was hunted because there was honour. There was a chance that you might not make it out of the hunt alive. I have been told that there was a law that men would not have sex for four days before they went on a hunt. Because animals sense human sexual energy. It's not ferocity you're going after. You're going in like with a cloak. You don't want your sexuality to be out there giving off warning signs. So, if you don't have that sexual energy, then you're not carrying that into the hunt. So as not to draw attention. They needed ᓲᐦᑲᐢᑤᐏᐣ sôhkastwâwin. That's a kind of attentiveness. A kind of listening. A kind of communication. A discipline.

Oh my. I was just thinking about that this morning. Like how they used to communicate before. Like from where we went. Where you took me to, that place. That nice place. Ribstone.[27] That's where they, the ᓀᐦᐄᔭᐘᐠ nêhîyawak, would have had their smoke signals. There on that hill and to some other high point. But I wonder how else they communicated. There had to be a line of communication somehow, I guess – runners, criers. Primarily runners. The nations were always in communication with each other. They were not always at odds with each other.

It was also against the law to kill female animals in the spring. Unless the people were starving. There were treaties with the animals – human-to-duck treaties, human-to-deer treaties.

27 The ribstone is a sacred site near the original place of ᒪᓂᑑᐤ ᐊᓯᓃᕀ manitôw asinîy and close to the town of Viking, Alberta.

And there was no war or strife allowed in certain areas. No one was allowed to live in certain areas, either.[28] For example, at ᒪᓂᑑᐤ ᓵᑳᐦᐃᑲᐣ manitôw sâkâhikan, manitôw lake or Lac Ste. Anne, no war or strife was allowed, and no one was allowed to go there at all, not en masse. Instead, they camped out at Devil's Lake. Don't know who came up with that name – not the neechies!

Good source of water there. During the day they would go out to Lac Ste. Anne. Healers with their helpers and the patients. But you couldn't make a camp out there at all.

No camping. You needed to leave the land without any indication that you had been there. You had to leave the land in as good condition or even better than how you found it. That's called ᒪᓈᒋᐦᐄᐍᐏᐣ manâcihîwêwin. Saving the grace and dignity of the land.

This is an example of how the people had treaty with the lands. ᒪᓂᑑᐤ ᓵᑳᐦᐃᑲᐣ manitôw lake, or Lac Ste. Anne, as it's come to be known, is another example of how the people had water treaties as well.

Also, where the rock fell, the ᒪᓂᑑᐤ ᐊᓯᓃᕀ manitôw asinîy, they could go there, but to have war there was against international law. At Viking ribstone, too. It was the same there, too. No wars were allowed. But at the ᒪᓂᑑᐤ ᐊᓯᓃᕀ manitôw asinîy, the meteorite, no war was allowed because of its healing powers.[29]

---

28 This was part of a presentation prepared by Reuben Quinn and Christine Stewart for the "Symposium on 'Freedom and Indigenous Constitutionalism,'" at John Borrows, Distinguished Visiting Speaker Series, "Reading Law, Reading Stories," March 9, 2021, University of Alberta.

29 Part of this teaching was published in Christine Stewart and Reuben Quinn, "This," *The Capilano Review* 3, no. 48 (Fall 2022): 27–31.

Before, when the old men and old ladies used to talk, everyone would be very quiet while another was talking. There was always someone who spoke last who summarized it all. Like Eric Tootoosis and Ron Lameman. They are getting old, though, and we are losing our old narrators. They would take turns talking, "ᐊᐦᐋᐤ ᑮᔭ ᐁᑿ" ahâw kîya êkwa, okay, you now." They wouldn't say the name of the person, but everyone would know who was next. Anyone who had been colonized (just like me!) would get confused and think that it was their turn when it wasn't.

There is a way of understanding in every culture. Like the question-and-answer thing. Questions would be asked by the people. The questions were at the beginning. The knowledge keepers would then discuss what questions had been asked, and they would discuss. The ᑮᐦᑌᐊᔭᐠ kîhtêayak, elders, would offer perspectives but not necessarily solutions. They would offer suggestions only if asked.

After treaty was broken, the Queen and the government had systems to keep track of us. Systems that worked in favour of the colonizer and against us. So, like my status card. It's a card about status, my number. Government issued. Like a prison number. Basically, that's how they keep track of us, right? And ostensibly the North West Mounted Police were created, and ᐃᔩᓇᐘᐠ îyînawak were told that they, the North West Mounted Police, were created to protect them from whisky traders. So, there's a big problem down at Cypress Hills, where the whisky traders wiped out a whole bunch of us turtle islanders over there.

So, they are saying that the North West Mounted Police were created to protect "Indians." And we believed them because it sounded sweet, the way they spoke. But it was disingenuous. That's the thing. It was made to sound like protection or cooperation or something. Yeah, and it wasn't. And here I question this to this day. If you look back at, like, the RCMP on my reserve, are they an occupying force? I would say so. If you go back to our systems, we had a word for police – ᓯᒫᑲᓂᐢ simâkanis, those were the ones that looked after, after the community. But now that's what they call the RCMP and any police, police person. I think Saysewahum Sylvia McAdam talked about that – ᓯᒫᑲᓂᐢ simâkanis – and how it has changed in colonized times. So, if it's a nation-to-nation agreement, Saddle Lake shouldn't have to deal with this occupying force. They should have their own police force, their ᓯᒫᑲᓂᓴᐠ simâkanisak. Historically, we had police. But based on a different paradigm. They were more like what your community workers would be today or trauma therapists. They had the authority to make decisions. Like, should the husband be going someplace else for now to let things cool off? Or else in the community, you know, if two males there are not getting along, then ᓯᒫᑲᓂᐢ the simâkanis would go in there, intervene, and resolve the situation.

So, treaties exist between us and the trees. The tree people are connected to each other; they have an obligation; they breathe out oxygen; they breathe in carbon dioxide. This is symbiosis between us and the tree people. ᔫᑎᐣ yôtin, the wind, is a teacher – ᐅᑮᓯᑰ okîsikôw, grandfather breath of life.

ᐋᔩᐚᐢᑎᐣ âyîwâstin – the absolute calm is yôtin's ᓃᓲᑌᐤ nîsôtêw, twin.

The universe is one organism.

From what I was told about our universe and its beginning, the supreme being created everything in its time. We re-enact that beginning in ceremony with ᓰᓰᑿᐣ sîsîkwan, that's that rattle. The ᓰᓰᑿᐣ sîsîkwan is rattled four times. Within those four rattling beats is that moment that supreme being created all time. This time (right now) was created then, at that moment.

So, the supreme being gives certain people the gift of prophecy to see those times.

I would like to tell a story about a prophecy I heard.

ᐊᐦᐋᐤ ᓂᐅᑑᑌᒥᑎᐠ ᑭᐊᑕᒥᐢᑳᑎᓈᐋᐤ ᐆᑌ ᐅᐦᒋᐦ ᐸᐦᐹᐢᑌᓈˣ ᐄᐅᐦᑕᑘᐍᒨᔮᐣ
ahâw niotôtêmitik ki atamiskâtinâwâw ôtê ohcih pahpâstênâhk î ohtatwewêmoyân
ahâw, my friends I greet you from over here, on pahpâstêw land is where I am speaking to you from.

Back in 1986, I think it was. Was with my brothers, Carl and Gerald. Late Gerald, he passed away in 2022. We went down to Rocky Mountain House area. West and then further down to Nordegg, ended up at Rocky Mountain House. Through the Kootenay Plains there. Wound up at the reserve called Sunchild there. So, we're kind of looking around, and we found this old man still living in a log shack, log cabin. ᐊᑕᐲᐩ atapîy, ᐊᑕᐲᐩ atapîy was his name. Late ᐊᑕᐲᐩ ᑳ ᑮ ᐃᑎᐦᐟ atapîy kâ kî itiht. Beautiful man. We went into his place. Really nice, clean place. He had his blanket. His bed was all clean, and his son was there. So, his son went off somewhere. Now he was an old man, this man. And we talked and he served us some bannock and some tea. Oh, that's nice. So, we had bannock and tea and he began to speak. About being in ᒫᑐᑎᓵᐣ mâtotisân, a sweat lodge. His involvement in ᒫᑐᑎᓵᐣ mâtotisân, the sweat lodge. I consider that man a prophet. He talked about what was to come. The prophecy that was told to him. And he said, he was told, ᑮᐢᐱᐣ ᐁᑳ ᓇᓂᑐᐦᑕᐦ ᑭᒎᐚᒥᓇᐤ kîspin ekâ nanitohtah kicôwâminaw, if he doesn't listen, our brother, ᑲᐱᒧᐦᑌᐘᐠ ᐊᐱᐢᒍᓯᓴᐠ kapimohtêwak apiscosisak, there'll be small tornadoes and he said, that's the warning. What I understand from the old man is that those little tornadoes are actually the big ones that we've been getting more frequently. They are the signs that an even bigger tornado is coming, bigger than anything we know. So big it makes those ones we get now seem small in comparison. That is what will happen, if those in power don't listen, if they keep taking from the earth the way they do.

That old man said, if he doesn't listen, if our brother doesn't listen,
"ᐁᑯᑕᐦ ᐁᑲᐧᐦ ᑮᐢᐱᐣ ᐁᑳ ᓇᓂᑐᐦᑕᐦᑭᐦ ᐁᑯᑕᐦ ᐁᑲᐧᐦ ᒥᓯᑑᐃᐧᓲᐤ ᑲᐱᒧᐦᑌᐤ
êkotah êkwah kîspin ekâ nanitohtahkih êkotah êkwah misitôwisôw ka pimohtêw."

If he doesn't listen, pay heed to the repeated warning, that is when the actual big tornado will travel the earth.

Like, change your attitude and your function on the earth. Alter it. So that's more equal balanced, he said. Because we're taking out all kinds of things in the past 150 years. And he said, what will happen, ᒥᓯᑑᐃᐧᓲᐤ misitôwisôw ᑲᐱᒧᐦᑌᐤ ᐁᑲᐧᐦ kapimohtêw êkwah, if our brother doesn't listen, then, after all these smaller tornadoes, ᐊᐱᐢᑎᓲᐃᐧᓴᐠ apistisôwisak, if he doesn't listen after these ones, these smaller ones come, ᐁᑯᑕᐦ ᐁᑲᐧᐦ ᒥᓯᑑᐃᐧᓲᐤ ᑲᐱᒧᐦᑌᐤ êkotah êkwah misitôwisôw kapimohtêw, there now, the big one, the cleansing one, will bring forth its life on the continent, on top of this continent, and clean it, clean this continent. If our brother doesn't listen, the big tornado, the cleansing one, will bring its life form, ᑲᐱᒧᐦᑌᐤ kapimohtêw.

Now, as I said before, most people will translate ᑲᐱᒧᐦᑌᐤ kapimohtêw as "walk," but ᐱᒼ pim means "life movement," and ᐱᒧᐦᑌ pimohtê means "life's movement on the land," and ᐱᒥᐦᐋ

pimihâ means "life's movement in the air." I talked about that contract between the trees and the wind, and the trees move that and it gives us life, ᐱᒧᐦᑌ pimohtê. And ᐱᒥᒋᒣ pimicimê, life's movement on the water, in the water, life's movement on the water.

So, getting back to this prophecy, this big tornado will save this land. If we don't listen, if we don't start reducing our carbon footprint.

ᐄᐱᐦᒋᐳᐦᑖᔭᕽ ᓂᐲᐩ
î pihcipohtâyahk nipîy
we are poisoning the water

ᐄᐱᐦᒋᐳᐦᐋᔭᐦ ᔫᑎᐣ
î pihcipohâyah yôtin
we are poisoning the wind

ᐄᐱᐦᒋᐳᐦᑖᔭᐦ ᐊᐢᑮᐩ
î pihcipohtâyah askîy
we are poisoning the earth

ᐄᐱᐦᒋᐳᐦᑖᔭᕽ îpihcipohtâyahk means "we are poisoning it."

We're introducing new and deadlier pollution into nature for the past 150 years. In a short geological time, we have done this to our earth. Now there needs to be a balance to bring that balance back. Was the same thing that happened with the other cleansings. So, that's going to be the air cleansing. That's going to happen. There have been quite a few cleansings, and most notorious are the fire cleansings. The water cleansings, too. Everybody has stories. Many people have stories about how the earth was flooded. So, there's been a water cleansing, and there's a story behind that, too. And then there's been the land cleansing. The earth's moving, moving. So, this one that's coming up is the air cleansing. So, there's cycles. So, that, that's one of the things that we're talking about, tornadoes.

ᐃᐢᑯᑌᐤ iskotêw has given us fire cleansing.
ᐊᐢᑮᐩ askîy has given us earth cleansing.
ᓂᐲᐩ nipîy has brought us water cleansing.
ᔫᑎᐣ yôtin will bring us air cleansing.

And on this earth, we just go through space. There is no escape. Wherever we go, here we are.
That's what I was talking about. Just looking at it from a realistic perspective. We're sitting in front of this computer monitor, and yet we're spinning at hundreds and hundreds of miles per hour. And don't even notice. We don't fly off. So, this earth loves us, embraces us. The earth's gravity pulls us and embraces us to her bosom,

ᑭᑳᐑᓇᐤ[30]

kikâwînaw, our mother – the earth.

So, yeah. There's a reason why ᐊᓯᓃᐩ asinîy, the stone, is so important in every culture, as well. ᐄᔩᓇᐤ îyînaw people have had ᐊᓯᓃᔭᐠ asinîyak, rocks, stories for millennia. And those are the ones that we find to be our relatives. We were told they're our relatives, and so a story I was told, that I don't mind repeating. By an old man. He told me. Should I say the old man's name? The late Joe Roan. So, the story goes. When this island began to get peopled. The creator of this place said, "we have to have some people to look after my two-legged children, to speak for them." And so, all the great spirits, ᔫᑎᐣ yôtin, the wind, ᐲᔦᓰᐤ

30 This is an alternate spelling.

pîyesôw, the thunderbird, ᒧᐢᑐᐢ mostos, the buffalo, ᐋᐸᑯᓰᐢ[31] âpakosîs, the mouse, ᑭᐦᐄᐤ kihîw, the eagle, ᑳᑿᐦ kâkwah, the porcupine, ᑭᐦᒋ ᐅᑮᓯᑰᐊᐧᐠ kihci okîsikôwak, all the great spirits, got together. So, everyone got together and they were to decide who was to speak for the human children. And so, they all started debating about who was to speak for the human children. They all had their justifications as to why they should be picked. They all had their merits. And the debate was getting heated when the creator intervened and said, "and I have decided that I will choose the one who will speak for ᓂᐅᑕᐋᐧᓯᒥᓴᐠ ni otawâsimisak, my children, the people, ᐋ ᔩᓰᔩᓇᐊᐧᐠ ayîsîyînawak, the two-legged people."

So, ᔫᑎᐣ yôtin, the wind, said, "I will speak for the people." And the creator said, "ᓇᒨᔭᐦ namôyah, no."

ᐲᔦᓲᐤ pîyesôw, the thunderbird, said, "I will speak."

And the creator said, "ᓇᒨᔭᐦ namôyah, no."

And all the great spirits offered, and the creator said, "ᓇᒨᔭᐦ namôyah."

Then ᒨᓴᐧᐦ môswah, the moose, said, "I will speak for the people."

And the creator said, "ᓇᒨᔭᐦ namôyah, moose, you will not speak for the people."

And the ᒨᓴᐧᐦ môswah got angry! And said, "why not?"

And the creator said, "because you have a bad temper."

31 Many say ᐋᐧᐸᑯᓰᐢ, but this is how we say it in Saddle Lake.

And ᒨᓴ·ᐦ môswah charged angrily. ᒨᓴ·ᐦ môswah just came charging at the creator, full gallop, and the creator is pushing back on the moose's head.

If you can see, I'm being animated right now where ᒨᓴ·ᐦ môswah is going, full gallop at the creator. Now the creator is pushing a hand back on the moose's head, pushing ᒨᓴ·ᐦ môswah back. And so, ᒨᓴ·ᐦ môswah was not the one to speak for the people. But if you look on the forehead of the moose, they say, you'll see the handprint of the creator there. Yeah.

So, then the divine mystery addressed ᐊᓯᓃ⁺ asinîy, the stone, and said,
"ᑮᔭᐦ ᑲᐲᑭᐢᑫ·ᐢᑕᒪᐋ·ᐊ·ᐠ
kîyah ka pîkiskwestamawâwak."
You will speak for my children.

And ᐊᓯᓃ⁺ asinîy said,
"ᑖᓂᐦᑭ ᓃᔭᐦ ᓇᒨᔭᐦ ᐄ·ᐦᑲ⁻ ᑮᑲ·⁺ ᐄᐋ·ᐸᐦᑕᒫᐣ
tânihki nîyah. namôyah wîhkac kîkway î wâpahtamân."
Why me? I never see anything.

That ᐊᓯᓃ⁺ asinîy is saying that he never goes anywhere, never sees anything, and he doesn't know what's happening.

And the creator said, "ᐁᐅ·ᑯᐦᒋ ᑮᔭ ewokohci kîya." That is exactly why it must be you to speak for the people, because you have humility.[32]

So, it came to be that the ᐊᓯᓃ⁺ asinîy spoke for the people in ᒦᑰᐋ·ᐦᐸᐦ mîkôwâhpah, the lodges, and in ᐅᐢᐸ·ᑲᐣ ospwâkan, the pipe, ᓰᓰᑲ·ᐣ sîsîkwan, the rattle, and other ceremonies. So, if you go in the ᒫᑐᑎᓵᐣ mâtotisân, sweat lodge, you'll see ᐊᓯᓃᔭᐠ

32 ᑖᑕᐸᐦᒋᒧᐠ tâtapahcimok. The fifth law, ᒥ (see glossary).

asinîyak, stones, in there where people send their messages to ᐊᓯᓃᔭᐠ asinîyak, the stones. The stone's purpose is to take that message and carry it into the ethereal, into the creator's realm. And same with the ᐅᐢᐋᐧᑲᐣ ospwâkan, pipe, ᐅᐢᐋᐧᑲᓇᐠ ospwâkanak, the pipes.

There were ᐅᐢᐋᐧᑲᓇᐠ ospwâkanak, pipes, here before contact.

The catlinite stone is a red pipestone, claystone, that is very malleable and easy to work with. It comes from a large pipestone quarry in Pipestone, Minnesota. After it comes from Pipestone, Minnesota, people will work and fashion that stone into a bowl for a pipe. That is how the pipestones are still made.

Anyways, so that's one of the legends. From one clan system. One system here on turtle island, on the view on how ᐊᓯᓃᐩ asinîy came to be so prominent in ᐄᔩᓈᐤ îyînaw life.

What's that guy's name again? From Manitoba. What's his name again? Wilfred Buck. According to him, we come from that star system. And I have been told that the little dipper represents the ᐃᐢᑵᐘᐠ iskwêwak pipe. When you're in the ᓂᐹᑵᓯᒨᐃᐧᑲᒥᐠ nipâkwêsimôwikamik, the sundance, you'll notice that the men will have these big long pipes and pass them around. And ᐃᐢᑵᐘᐠ iskwêwak, they'll have ᐅᐢᐋᐧᑲᓂᐢ ospwâkanis, a little tiny pipe like that, passing that around. ᐅᐢᐋᐧᑲᓂᐢ ospwâkanis, that little pipe, is the one, that's the power as well. And ᐃᐢᑵᐘᐠ iskwêwak always smoke. It's a law. We have to follow that law. Half of the lodge belongs to the females and half belongs to men. I don't know if "belong" is the right word.

And what ᐄᔩᓇᐘᐠ îyînawak, turtle islanders, realized a long time ago, at the beginning, was that they needed water to sustain the lands and all the other nations. The ᓀᐦᐄᔭᐘᐠ nêhîyawak would call upon ᐲᔦᓲᐤ pîyesôw, their friend, their backup, ᑭᐅᑑᑌᒼ kiotôtêm, their otôtêm.

ᐅᑑᑌᒼ otôtêm, they're someone who's going to back you up. Like when you go to the store, you know, and your mom doesn't want to you to buy any candy, but your granny's there, your granny's your backup. So, you can nudge your granny, and she'll get you something. So, it's like that. You have a backup. You have a backup in that, that being. Just like you have a backup in a person. So, we call that relationship ᐚᐦᑯᐦᑑᐏᐣ wâhkohtôwin.

ᐄ ᐚᐦᑯᒥᐟ ᐲᔦᓲᐤ î wâhkomit pîyesôw. What that means is that they are making you their relative, and you are making them your relative.

So, if you were to put ᐅᑑᑌᒼ otôtêm and exclude that first vowel sound, and anglicize it, you would be reading the word, "totem." Well, what is in a totem? It's just the same thing. What would you expect from that? Some type of, ah, comfort, right? Relief, whatever, from that being. That's ᑭᐅᑑᑌᒼ kiotôtêm, your friend, your ally. ᓂᐅᑑᑌᒼ niotôtêm is my friend, my ally. But everybody had an ᐅᑑᑌᒼ otôtêm. Everyone still has one.

If you go and see Wilfred Buck, he'll start talking about ᐊᐄᐧᓇ awîna, who are his, his ᐅᑑᑌᒪᐦ otôtêmah. I think he lists more than three or maybe four or five or six. I don't remember now. But there are quite a few. Now those ᐅᑑᑌᒪᐦ otôtêmah in the spiritual realm perform the function that is given them by the creative intelligence. For ᐲᔦᓲᐤ pîyesôw, that is to look after water.

The people build ᑳᒥᓴᐠ ᒦᑰᐚᐦᑊ kâmisak mîkôwâhp, the big lodge, a huge lodge. Made out of sometimes up to fifteen poles. They get the ᐅᑭᒫᐚᐦᑎᐠ okimâwâhtik, the centre pole. There they make a nest and then they build the lodge around that. That lodge, that is our home.

When it's finished, you know, it's all covered up with leafy trees, and in the centre you have that pole.

And before they put that pole up, they get willows for the nest, and those are the willows that the scouts gathered on the morning that they go out to get ᐅᑭᒫᐚᐦᑎᐠ okimâwâhtik, the boss tree. They wear those willows as camouflage. They camouflage their bodies with those willows when they are coming back into the camp. And those willows are what makes up that ᐘᒋᐢᑑᐘᐣ wacistôwan, the nest, on the top of the ᐅᑭᒫᐚᐦᑎᐠ okimâwâhtik, the boss tree, the sundance tree.

Nothing is wasted, and as far as that nest is concerned, they try to think of what would be the most opportune way to entice ᐲᔦᓲᐤ pîyesôw, the thunderbird, to bring water and other blessings.

So, there's a connection with what the scouts do on ᒪᐦᐄᐦᑲᐣ ᒣᐢᑲᓇᐤ mahîhkan meskanaw, the wolf's trail, and the ᐅᑭᒫᐚᐦᑎᐠ okimâwâhtik, the boss tree, the sundance tree. ᒪᐦᐄᐦᑲᐣ ᒣᐢᑲᓇᐤ mahîhkan meskanaw, the wolf's trail, is the Milky Way, and then the men are re-enacting what the wolves do.

After the lodge is built, there is a ceremony, and ᐅᓵᑭᑑᐤ osâkitôw, the crier, will go around the camp and announce to the people, "ᐯᑮᐍᐠ pê kîwek, come home!" Those who pledge to dance line up with their camping gear around the ᓂᐹᑫᓯᒨᐃᐧᑲᒥᐠ nipâkwêsimôwikamik. After that, they go into the lodge and stay in there for the next four days without food or water.

In ᓀᐦᐄᔭᐁᐧᐃᐧᐣ nêhîyawêwin, that lodge is called ᓂᐹᑫᐧᓯᒨᐃᐧᑲᒥᐠ nipâkwêsimôwikamik. ᓂᐹᑫᐧ nipâkwe means "to go without any liquid touching your throat." No liquid to touch the dancer's throat for whatever amount of time. Just their spit. Probably. They get thirsty, they start swallowing their spit. Anyways, that's what ᓂᐹᑫᐧ nipâkwe means, nothing, no water to go into your throat, and ᓯᒨᐤ simôw is how one moves in this ᓂᐹᑫᐧ nipâkwe way. Your movement is your prayer. Instead of your mouth, your body becomes the voice of your prayer. ᓯᒨᐤ simôw means "to placate, to entice, to plead with your body and with the whistle."

ᓃᒦᐦ nîmîh means "to implore with your body."
ᐄᓃᒦᐦᐋᔭᐦ ᐊᐑᔭᐠ
î nîmîhâyah awîyak
to implore someone (with your body's movement)

Specifically, the way they dance in ᓂᐹᑫᐧᓯᒨᐃᐧᑲᒥᐠ nipâkwêsimôwikamik is ᓂᐹᑫᐧᓯᒨᐤ nipâkwêsimôw, and that means "to move your body, to implore with your body and with your entire being."

With ᐱᐱᑲᐧᐣ pipikwan, the whistle, the dancer calls to ᐅᑭᒫᐤ ᐲᔦᓲᐤ okimâw pîyesôw while going without water or food for four days. And that ᐱᐱᑲᐧᐣ pipikwan expresses what your body, your mind, your spirit, and your emotions are going through in ᓂᐹᑫᐧᓯᒨᐃᐧᑲᒥᐠ nipâkwêsimôwikamik.

ᓯᒨᐤ simôw is also the rhythmic way one moves to the beat of the ᓰᓰᑲᐧᐣ sîsîkwan, the rattle, and ᒥᐢᑎᑲᐧᐢᑮᐦᑲᐧᐠ mistikwaskîhkwak, the drums. In that ᓰᓰᑲᐧᐣ sîsîkwan, that rattle, is the universe and the beat of ᒥᐢᑎᑲᐧᐢᑮᕽ mistikwaskîhk, the drum, is the earth's beat. I have been told that that beat is in 7/8 time and birds sing in 7/8 time. So, in ᓂᐹᑫᐧᓯᒨᐃᐧᑲᒥᐠ nipâkwêsimôwikamik, in the dance, in the ᓂᐹᑫᐧᓯᒨᐃᐧᑲᒥᐠ nipâkwêsimôwikamik, the sundance, they dance like this, up and down in 7/8 time, and they have a very important tool that was given them to communicate with the ethereal and also pragmatically with ᐋᔦᓲᐤ pîyesôw, the thunderbird, a gift that was given them. That gift is ᐱᐱᑿᐣ pipikwan, the eagle whistle. And that ᐱᐱᑿᐣ pipikwan is the sound that ᐋᔦᓲᐤ pîyesôw is listening for. The grandfathers, grandmothers, and ᐋᔦᓲᐊᐠ pîyesôwak are listening for that. And they will come and answer. So, you send ᑳᑮᔨᓯᒨᐏᐣ kâkîyisimôwin, your prayer, as you are dancing. Can you hear that ᔨ yi? Today, the way people say it is a shortened version, ᑳᑮᓯᒨᐏᐣ kâkî'simowin.

So, we are missing that ᔨ yi and that is the eight law. That ᔨ is ᒪᓈᒌᐦᐃᑐᐠ manâcîhitok, to look at each other with care and tenderness, saving each other's grace, saving each other's dignity. And so when we leave out that syllable, we lose that law emanating from that word, ᑳᑮᔨᓯᒨᐏᐣ kâkîyisimôwin.

So, when you are blowing ᐱᐱᑿᐣ pipikwan, that whistle, you are conveying to that whistle your prayer, your thought, and you're calling upon that ᐋᔦᓲᐤ pîyesôw, the thunder being, for some kind of sustenance to carry you through a hard time. Maybe it's actual rain. Which is what we usually need. But in the nest on the ᐅᑭᒫᐋᐦᑎᐠ okimâwâhtik, the thunderbird, that's where it comes to rest.

It's ᒪᒫᐦᑖᐤ mamâhtâw, amazing to be there. This is a shift in your being.

Everybody comes into the lodge. Ants, bees, this little wiggly worm, crawling up to a leaf and then making a cocoon, and then getting out of there and flying and flying. Amazing. From ᒧᐦᑌᐤ mohtêw, worm, to ᑲᒫᒪᐠ kamâmak, a butterfly. ᑲᒫᒪᐠ kamâmak flying in the ᓂᐹᑵᓯᒨᐏᑲᒥᐠ nipâkwêsimôwikamik, the sundance lodge. That's ᒪᒫᐦᑖᐤ mamâhtâw, amazing. It helps people recognize the transformation of life. That's ᒪᒫᐦᑖᐤ mamâhtâw. I remember what Randy told me about Noah's ᓂᐹᑵᓯᒨᐏᑲᒥᐠ nipâkwêsimôwikamik, sundance, and how a butterfly came in. And then I guess Noah had the biggest smile. He was just happy. Another year, at the end of ᓂᐹᑵᓯᒨᐏᑲᒥᐠ nipâkwêsimôwikamik, there was a big clap of thunder, and again he had that big smile and was very happy.

Yeah so, there's a lot of community that happens in building ᑳᒥᓴᐠ ᒦᑰᐚᐦᑊ kâmisak mîkôwâhp, the big lodge. That's one of the things. You build something, and the people will come too if it has a practical purpose. One practical function of ceremony is to get people together and create community. And with community you have power. And you have the prayer of each individual, which is even more powerful. So, it has a pragmatic function that ᓂᐹᑵᓯᒨᐏᑲᒥᐠ nipâkwêsimôwikamik, that sundance lodge, bringing community together at least once a year. Some relatives, I heard, when they married away, they would only see each other not very frequently. But with the ᓂᐹᑵᓯᒨᐏᑲᒥᐠ nipâkwêsimôwikamik, the sundance, they get to see each other at least once a year. Right. So that has a practical function.

And you get to connect with ᐲᔦᓲᐤ pîyesôw. That's the important thing, and that ethereal function is depending upon the ancestors and the sacred helping spirits – like ᒧᐢᑐᐢ mostos, the buffalo, ᐲᔦᓲᐤ pîyesôw, the thunderbird, ᑭᐦᐄᐤ kihîw, the eagle, ᒪᐢᑿ maskwa, the bear.

ᐅᐢᑳᐯᐏᓴᐠ oskâpêwisak, the two-legged helpers, get everything ready for this holy event. As participants, the sacred ground has been prepared and our part in it is to be willing. The rest is up to us. As an example, that is what I say to the people when they come to ᒫᑐᑎᓵᐣ mâtotisân – "the helpers have made the fire, heated the rocks, got the fish and the berries and the tea and prepared the lodge. Now the rest is up to us to connect with the holy creator and all the sacred helping spirits."

The ethereal function, and I wish knew those words that had to do with the energy that comes from something that used to be living but that goes into the other realm. We go into the other realm after we expire from this body, this vestibule, we will go into a different realm. I've forgotten what that's called again. But that's exactly what we rely on in ᓂᐹᑫᐧᓯᒨᐃᐧᑲᒥᑲᐧᐦ nipâkwêsimôwikamikwah, sundances.

So, ᓂᐹᑫᐧᓯᒨᐃᐧᑲᒥᑲᐧᐦ nipâkwêsimôwikamikwah, sundances, have a practical function. They bring community together. And then there's the people that hear about the ᓂᐹᑫᐧᓯᒨᐃᐧᑲᒥᐠ nipâkwêsimôwikamik, the sundance, and they want to be part of that as well. So, the community grows from a little hamlet, you know, where the people are all the family, the helpers getting together. Pretty soon, after a while, you have a little town, and after a while, you have a little city. So, you know, it brings together community in a great way. That ᓂᐹᑫᐧᓯᒨᐃᐧᑲᒥᐠ nipâkwêsimôwikamik, that sundance, has a practical function, and the ethereal function of course is all the dancers and each individual asking ᐲᔦᓲᐤ pîyesôw, the thunderbird, who is a messenger of the creative intelligence. ᐲᔦᓲᐤ pîyesôw is given ᒪᓂᑑᐤ manitôw, power, to be the one who looks after the water. So that is the one that we try to connect with ethereally through ᐱᐱᑲᐧᐣ pipikwan, that whistle, with the help of ᓰᓰᑲᐧᐣ sîsîkwan, ᒥᐢᑎᑲᐧᐢᑮᕽ mistikwaskîhk, and of course the songs.

Some lodges are a little different structurally, but they are all based on the same idea, to get an ᐆᑐᑌᒼ otôtêm, an ᐅᑮᓯᑰᐤ okîsikôw, to help. Some people call upon ᒧᐢᑐᐢ mostos, the buffalo, as their ᐅᑑᑌᒼ otôtêm.

And ᑮᐦᑌᐊᔭᐠ kîhtêayak, the elders, speak there to remind people. What do they remind people of? How to function, how to live, how to be. They talk a lot about how to treat each other with ᑮᐦᒉᔩᐦᑑᐏᐣ kîhcêyîhtôwin, respect, and ᒪᓈᒌᐦᐃᑑᐏᐣ manâcîhitôwin, grace. That is what they talk about all the time. They talk about ᑖᐳᐘᑫᔩᐦᑕᒨᐏᐣ tâpowakeyîhtamôwin, faith or belief, and how important that is.

The holiest of the holy places is ᓂᐹᑵᓯᒨᐏᑲᒥᑯᐦ nipâkwêsimôwikamikoh. And, as I understand it, in ᓂᐹᑵᓯᒨᐏᑲᒥᐠ nipâkwêsimôwikamik, that lodge's structure, that's where ᐊᑖᐦᑭᐯᔩᐦᑲᓇᐠ atâhkipêyîhkanak, the spirit markers, are related. And it is also related to ᐅᐢᐚᑲᓂᐢ ospwâkanis, the little pipe that ᐃᐢᑵᐊᐧᐠ iskwêwak carry. This is also embodied in the chart – in the image of the little dipper. It's such an intricate system that ᓂᐹᑵᓯᒨᐏᑲᒥᐠ nipâkwêsimôwikamik, that sundance lodge, as they call it.

And everyone is always welcome in the ᓂᐹᑵᓯᒨᐏᑲᒥᑯᐦ nipâkwêsimôwikamikoh, the sundance, and although I can't talk about so many things here, they are too sacred, there are ᑮᐦᑌᐊᔭᐠ kîhtêayak, elders, out there who can guide you. You can go and visit them, take ᒋᐢᑌᒫᐤ cistêmâw, some tobacco, and ask them.

I am not talking for all ᑮᐦᑌᐊᔭᐠ kîhtêayak, but a lot of elders like it when someone comes to visit them. There is so much more to learn and observe. There are also ceremony people, helpers who are only too happy to help. You can ask them, too. Everyone is willing to share if you ask them.

ᑕᑳᑭᐦ takâkih, it is awesome.

As we speak, ᓃᑎᒼ nîtim, I'm very fascinated with what's happening with our universe. Right now, we are spinning around the sun. Our earth, our beautiful mother, is spinning around the sun at 67,000 miles an hour, and our little solar system. It's flying through ᒪᐦᐄᐦᑲᐣ ᒣᐢᑲᓈᐤ mahîhkan meskanaw, the wolf's trail, the Milky Way galaxy, at 194 miles per second.

ᒪᒫᐦᑖᐏᐦ mamâhtâwih! How we can just hang on!
ᐃᐢᑫᔮᐨ iskweyâc
ᐋ ᓴᐍᔨᒼ ᑲᐦᑮᔭᐤ ᓂᐗᐦᑰᒫᑲᓇᐠ
â sawêyim kahkîyaw niwahkômâkanak
holiest of holies bless all my relations

I just get amazed when I look at that chart, it reminds me.

For me, everything begins again and again, with the language. Each time I hear ᓀᐦᐃᔭᐍᐏᐣ nêhîyawêwin, it shifts my thinking, and the spirit markers are my foundation for understanding my ᓀᐦᐃᔭᐤ nêhîyaw language.

All of the information for a good life is held within the principles or laws of ᐊᑖᐦᑭᐯᔩᐦᑲᓇᐠ atâhkipêyîhkanak, the spirit markers, and in that chart they make up.

As a ᓀᐦᐃᔭᐤ nêhîyaw nonfluent speaker, that is where I feel most comfortable, talking about the language and the spirit marker's laws.

They are everything I aspire to be ˣ, to be home.

ᐁᑯᑕᐦ ᐱᑕᒫ êkotah pitamâ
ᐯᑮᐍᐠ pê kîwek, come home

Acknowledgments

First and foremost, ᐋ, the supreme being.

My biggest cultural teacher was Maurice Quinn, my father. Thanks to him.

My father always spoke to me in ᓀᐦᐄᔭᐤ nêhîyaw. He didn't know much English. I learned from my brother, Carl Quinn, language and cultural teachings. I learned from my brother, Clifford Cardinal. I fasted under him for eight to ten years and Noah Cardinal. Noah was a ceremony man, his dad was a ceremony man – they talked in the old way, and Albert Pasquayak was my cultural teacher. The late Victoria Cardinal taught me about ᓀᐦᐄᔭᐤ nêhîyaw religion. I have been given ceremonies: grandmother buffalo lodge, various pipe directions, by different ᑮᐦᑌᐊᔭᐠ kîhtêayak, elders. I danced under Noah Cardinal and Dewey Dion. I danced nonconsecutively in the ᓀᐦᐄᔭᐤ nêhîyaw dances. I danced at Saddle Lake, Alberta, under Noah Cardinal (ᓀᐦᐄᔭᐤ nêhîyaw). The following year I danced (Blackfeet) in Browning, Montana, under Buster Yellow Kidney (Blackfeet sundance man) and danced (Nakoda) at Fort Belknap, Montana, under John Allen for four years. The following year I danced (ᓀᐦᐄᔭᐤ nêhîyaw) at Sweet Grass, Saskatchewan, under Joe Roan. I danced at Frog Lake, Alberta, under Dewey Dion. Danced for the final year at Saddle Lake, Alberta, (ᓀᐦᐄᔭᐤ nêhîyaw) under Noah Cardinal. Then I danced under Joe Fourstar in Wahpeyton, Saskatchewan, for seven years.

My brother Gerald was taught by Uncle Jim kâ-nîpitêhtêw (from *The Counselling Speeches of Jim Kâ-Nîpitêhtêw*), and I learned some things from him through my brother. I got my language teachings in Saddle Lake in 1971 from Rosanna Houle, who taught me the spirit markers, and Caroline Hunter. They learned from the late Peter Shirt, ᐲᐦᐁᐤ pîhêw, old, old man in 1970. I also learned the spirit markers through Joe Redcrow and Joe McGilvery. All my ceremony brothers are leaving me. Pipe ceremonies were passed on to me from different ᑮᐦᑌᐊᔭᐦ kîhtêayah, elders. An eight-pole ᒫᑐᑎᓵᐣ mâtotisân, sweat lodge, was passed on to me by Joe Roan with teachings like the stone teachings. The late George Bretton sang me out to a fast, and I learned about ceremony from him. So many teachers, including the ones that are currently helping me – Dave Culpen, Trevor Gladue, Dan Sheehan, Ian Gladue, Kyra Brown, and Heather Bessey. I am grateful to them for helping me live. I want to thank all these people, my former students and countless others, including four-legged friends and winged ones, for keeping me alive.

I want to thank Christine Stewart, Courteney Morin, Savage Bear, Angela Van Essen, Roberta Alook, Keavy Martin, Deneh'Cho Thompson, Graeme Comyn, and Kaitlyn Purcell. ᐊᔩᐦᐊᐩ âyîhay to the Edmonton Heritage Council for generously supporting this book through the Funding Indigenous Resurgence in Edmonton (FIRE) grant.

I would also like to acknowledge ᓂᑳᐑᐸᐣ nikâwîpan, ᐅᑮᐦᒉᔩᐦᑘᐏᐢᑵᐤ o kîhcêyîhtwâwiskwêw née Elizabeth Josephine Houle and nitânis, ᐅᒐᐲᐦᑫᐤ ocapîhkêw, Elizabeth, who now takes on the adult name of her grandmother, ᐅᑮᐦᒉᔩᐦᑘᐏᐢᑵᐤ o kîhcêyîhtwâwiskwêw.

Glossary

Note on Pronunciation

Regarding the long and short vowels, you will hear and see discrepancies due to vowel reduplication in certain contexts. Additionally, you might also hear older people carefully enunciating with longer vowels.

ᐋ â

supreme being

ᐋ â is how all ᓀᐦᐄᔭᐤ nêhîyaw will call upon the supreme being. It is the first sound uttered before invoking the sacred spirits.

ᐋᔩ âyî

supreme being

I have been told that this was the name prior to contact.

ᐊᒑᐦᑭᐯᔩᐦᑲᓂᓴᐠ acâhkipêyîhkanisak

the small spirit markers

ᐊᑖᐦᑭᐯᔩᐦᑲᓇᐠ atâhkipêyîhkanak

spirit markers

ᐊᑖᕽ atâhk

spirit or star

ᐊᑖᐦᑳᐧᐠ atâhkwâk

spirits or stars

ᐊᐋᐧᐦᐁ awahê

Something like, "as you travel, I wish for you to see good things, that you will travel safe, that you will be blessed on your journey home, and that when you arrive, you will bring all of those good blessings through your door with you and into your home."

ᐊᐑᓈᐦ ᐄᐃᑌᐧᐟ awînah î itwet

who said it?

ᐋᔩᑭᐢ âyîkis

frog

An alternate spelling is ᐋᔩᑭᐢ.

ᐋᔩᒪᐣ âyîman

challenging times, it is difficult, it is challenging

ᐋᔩᓰᔩᓇᐘᐠ âyîsîyînawak

the two-legged people

We come from the breath of ᐋ â – ᐄᔩᑯᐲᐑᐤ îyîkopîwîw, the fog, or mist, or steam.

ᒌᑭᓈᕽ cîkinâhk

parasite

ᐃᓄᑎᑵᐟ inotikwet

Child tending by the older or physicaly challenged ladies in the community who were unable to do strenuous physical tasks. This is where the words ᓅᑎᑵᐤ nôtikwêw and ᓅᒋᑵᓲᐤ nôcikwêsôw come from.

ᐃᐢᑵᐤ iskwêw

This is the one who determines future generations. A prophet can prophesize the future. You have the ability to foretell, to shape the future. Something like a forecaster. ᐅᑭᐢᑯᐍᐦᐃᑫᐤ okiskowêhikêw. The word ᐃᐢᑵᐤ iskwêw, female, comes from this concept – from the verb ᑭᐢᑯᐍᐦ kiskowêh – (prophesy). ᐄᑭᐢᑰᐍᐦᐃᑫᐟ îkiskôwêhikêt, she is prophesying. ᐃᐢᑵᐤ iskwêw have the bodily capability to prophesize the future.

ᐄᐑᒉᐢᑰᐘᑭᓂᑯᔭᕽ îwîcêskôwakinikoyahk

Someone (the supreme being, in this case) is moulding us

ᐄᔩᑯᐲᐑᐤ îyîkopîwîw

the earth's fog or mist

We come from that. That fog, that mist, completes our human-ness. The first thing that ᐋ â will do is give us that breath, that fog that brings us to life after we are moulded. Who is moulding us? That is ᐋ â or the supreme being.

ᐄᔩᓇᐘᐠ îyînawak

two-legged people

The morpheme ᐄᔩᐢ îyîs that breath of life, that earth's fog that is blown into us for completion.

ᐄᔩᐘᓂᓰᔩᓲᐏᐣ îyîwanisîyîsôwin

fasting

ᑳᑮᔩᓯᒧᐦ kâkîyîsimoh

to pray

Literally it means "to placate, to sooth, to plead with praise." To pray in a humble manner.

ᑭᐢᑯᐦᐊᐚᓲᐤ kiskohawâsôw

to be with child, to be cloaked and suffused in the stardust, star spirit energy of that being

ᑮᓯᐠ kîsik

a sacred spirit

ᑭᐢᑭᓯᐦ kiskisih

(you) remember

ᑭᐢᑭᓱᒥᑐᐠ kiskisomitok

to remind each and one another

ᑭᐢᑯᓅᐚᒌᐦᒋᑲᐣ kiskonôwâcîhcikan

a map, a legend, a medicine wheel

This is the proper way, but I say ᑭᐢᑰᓄᐚᒌᐦᒋᑲᐣ iskônowâcîhcikan, which leaves out one spirit marker. I am trying to correct this. When I remember!

ᑭᐢᑌᔩᐦᑐᑖᐣ kistêyîhtotân

let's show each other consideration and respect

ᑭᔮᒼ kiyâm

letting go, trusting in a power beyond our own, and being quiet in that letting go, to quiet yourself and let things go and leave them there

Come back to the present and don't bring back those turmoils.

ᒪᓈᒌᔩᑐᐠ manâcîyîtok

the concept and law of "civility"

To respect each and every one. This is a law, the twenty-third law. On one level, it means "to save each other" or to be civil to each other, saving another's grace. On another level, ᒪᓈᒌᔩᑐᐠ manâcîyîtok means, in part, leaving things the way you found them or in better condition. When I say "things," I mean humans, too. We leave others as they were or in even better condition; it means being civil to all your nonhuman and human relations. ᒪᓈᑎᓲᐏᐣ manâtisôwin is civility. Nowadays you might hear ᒪᓈᐟᐢᐏᐣ manât's'win instead. But you lose the flavour of the word, ᒪᓈᑎᓲᐏᐣ manâtisôwin. The old people would emphasize the word by making a reduplicate within the vowel. In this case, that reduplicate is a long ᐆ ô, ᒪᓈᑎᓲᐏᐣ manâtisôwin, emanating kindness. I remember hearing it that way. I remember the kindness. It is the same with today's pronunciation of ᓵᑮᔩᑑᐏᐣ sâkîyîtôwin. Now, it is often said as ᓴᑮᐩᐟᐏᐣ sakîy't'win. Whereas the old people used the long vowels sounds to give the feeling of the word, ᓵᑮᔩᑑᐏᐣ sâkîyîtôwin.

ᒪᓂᑑᐤ manitôw
creator

ᒪᓂᒎᐢ manicôs
little creator

ᒫᑐᑎᓵᐣ mâtotisân or ᐚᑭᓄᒁᐣ wâkinokwân, a bent lodge
the sweat lodge

ᒫᑐᐦ mâtoh
to cry
The sweat lodge is a place for tears of pain, gratitude, and happiness.

ᒣᒧᐦᒑᕽ mêmohcâhk
fart spirit

ᒥᓯᑭᓈᕽ misikinâhk
turtle

ᒥᐢᑮᓯᐠ miskîsik
spirit finder, spirit detector, or eye, as it is simply called

It is the morpheme ᑮᓯᐠ kîsik, within ᒥᐢᑮᓯᐠ miskîsik in this context that makes ᒥᐢᑮᓯᐠ miskîsik a sacred spirit finder.

ᒥᐢᑮᓯᑿᐦ miskîsikwah
eyes, plural
We find the day as a spiritual event through ᒥᐢᑮᓯᑿᐦ miskîsikwah, eyes.

ᒥᐢᑕᒣᒫᑲᓇᐠ mistamêmâkanak
the ancestors

ᓂᐢᑕᒣᒫᑲᓇᐠ nistamêmâkanak
my ancestors

ᑭᐢᑕᒣᒫᑲᓇᐠ kistamêmâkanak
your ancestors

ᒦᔪᐢᑲᒦᕽ mîyoskamîhk
in the spring

ᒦᔪᐚᑕᒧᐠ mîyowâtamok
the third law, have fun/be joyful

ᒨᒋᑮᐦᑖᑖᐣ môcikîhtâtân
let's have fun!

ᓀᐦᐄᔭᐘᐠ nêhîyawak
the ᓀᐦᐄᔭᐤ nêhîyaw people

ᓃᐱᐣ nîpin
summer

ᓃᐱᓰᐘᓴᐢᑵᐦᑑᐤ nîpisîwasaskwehtôw
willow fungus

ᓂᐢᑐᐦᑕ nistohtah

understanding on three levels – what was said, what was heard, and what was understood between two parties – to always consider something greater and outside ourselves We all have two ears. ᒦᐦᑕᐘᑲᐩ mîhtawakay, ear, so when we are told ᓂᐢᑐᐦᑕᒧᐠ nistohtamok, we are asked to listen with our ear, ᓇᓇᐦᐄᐦᑕᐘᑲᔦ nanahîhtawakaye – which is a reduplicate, it has emphasis. What it's really asking us is to listen with our third ear, our heart. I heard that our heart has the abstract shape of our ear. ᓂᐢᑐᐦᑕᒧᐠ nistohtamok, to listen with the heart, to perceive from a third level.

ᐅᒉᐦᑲᑕᕽ ocehkatahk

martin fisher spirit, the name for the north star

ᐅᐦᒋᑯᐚᐴᐏᐣ ohcikowâpôwin

the unforced teardrop of gratitude
This is the greatest gift.

ᐅᒫᓂᑌᐤ omânitew

guest

ᐅᑕᐲᐦᑫᐤ otapîhkêw

the weaver or spider, as it is known

ᐯᔮᐦᑎᐠ pêyâhtik

take it slow, take it easy

ᐸᐯᔮᐦᑎᐠ papêyâhtik

really take it easy

ᐲᒋᒌᐏᐣ pîcicîwin

now known as the round dance

To be within each other's hand clasp, holding each other, the movement with the arms swinging as ᓃᒦᐦᑐᐦ nîmîhitoh, as you dance to the movement of the song(s).

ᐱᒼ pim
a dependent morpheme, meaning life

ᐱᒫᒋᐦᐃᐍᐏᐣ pimâcihiwêwin
giving of life

ᐱᒫᑎᓲᐏᐣ pimâtisôwin
life, it encompasses all of our lives

ᐱᒥᒋᒣ pimicimê
life's movement in or on water

ᐱᒥᐦᐋ pimihâ
life's movement in the air

ᐱᒧᐦᑌ pimohtê
life's movement on the earth

ᐱᐳᐣ pipon
winter

ᓵᑭᐸᑳᐤ sâkipakâw
when the buds are coming out, unfurling, the grass beginning to grow
That is what the earth does, it emanates, it awakens the senses. That is also where we get the morpheme for love – ᓵᑭ sâki.

ᓵᑮᔩᑐᐠ sâkîyîtok
the first law, love each and one another

ᓴᕀᐍᔨᒼ saweyim

bless him, her, or it (animate)

ᓲᐦᑲᐢᑖᐠ sôhkastwâk

the fourth law: that's plural, you all make it strong, you all be disciplined

ᓲᐦᑲᐢᑖ sôhkastwâ is singular.

ᑕᒁᑭᐣ takwâkin

autumn

ᑖᓂᓯ ᑮᔭᐦ tânisi kîyah

a greeting, how are you?

The "are" is inferred.

ᑕᐸᐦᑌᔩᒧᐠ tapahtêyîmok

to have humility, to hold each other in esteem

As my brother, Carl Quinn, explains, the last part, "mok" (ᒧᐠ) refers to speech/sound. The first part, "tapah," means "low," i.e. to the earth. The middle part refers to how we perceive, conduct ourselves. This is usually translated as speaking with humility. Carl teaches that this is one of the laws, the fifth law, ᒥ. It's related to the word ᑕᐸᐦᑌᔨᒥᓱᐎᐣ tapahtêyimisowin, which is translated into English as "humility," to have humility, to speak, to pray, and to converse in a humble way. Think about how a mouse runs along low to the ground and does not grasp at loftier ways of being. Like a mouse, running along close to the ground, don't get too abstract! The ᐠ (k) ending means that this is an imperative, because it is a law and because it has a plural ending, it applies to each and every one of us, to all of us two-legged beings, two-legged people.

ᐘᐍᔩᐏᐣ waweyîwin
the twenty-seventh law, be prepared

ᐑᒌᔨᑐᐠ wîcîyitok
the second law, help each and one another

ᐑᐦᑫᐢ wîhkês
rat root

ᐁᑯᑕᐦ

êkotah

Good resources that you might like to follow up with

Amiskwaciy History Series. *YouTube*. Accessed October 8, 2024. www.youtube.com/@AmiskwaciyHistorySeries.

Borrows, John. "Distinguished Visiting Speaker Series 2021: Dr. John Borrows." Arts Resource Centre. March 9, 2021. *YouTube* video. 1 hour, 31 min. www.youtube.com/watch?v=VwTFQRexkd0.

Borrows, John. "Earth-Bound: Indigenous Law and Environmental Reconciliation." In *Resurgence and Reconciliation: Indigenous–Settler Relations and Earth Teachings*, edited by Michael Asch, John Borrows, and James Tully. University of Toronto Press, 2018.

Borrows, John. "Wampum at Niagara: Canadian Legal History, Self-Government, and the Royal Proclamation." In *Aboriginal and Treaty Rights in Canada: Essays on Law, Equality, and Respect for Difference,* edited by Michael Asch. UBC Press, 1998.

Edmonton Public Library. "Aboriginal History Documents (Papaschase)." www2.epl.ca/edmontonacitycalledhome/Papaschase.cfm.

Harp, Samara mîkiwin. "Origins of Cree Syllabics." *Library and Archives Canada Blog*. March 9, 2023. thediscoverblog.com/2023/03/09/origins-of-cree-syllabics/.

McAdam, Sylvia (Saysewahum). *Nationhood Interrupted: Revitalizing nêhiyaw Legal Systems*. UBC Press, 2015.

McNally, Conor, dir. *nipiy*. 2020. 3 min., 10 sec.

McNally, Conor, dir. *ôtênaw.* 2017. 40 min.

Stevenson (Wheeler), Winona. "Calling Badger and the Symbols of the Spirit Language: The Cree Origins of the Syllabic System." *Oral History Forum* 19–20 (1999–2000): 19–24.

Venne, Sharon. "Treaties Made in Good Faith." In *Natives and Settlers Now and Then: Historical Issues and Current Perspectives on Treaties and Land Claims in Canada*, edited by Paul W. DePasquale. University of Alberta Press, 2007.

Venne, Sharon. "Understanding Treaty 6: An Indigenous Perspective." In *Aboriginal and Treaty Rights in Canada: Essays on Law, Equality, and Respect for Difference,* edited by Michael Asch. UBC Press, 1998.

Great-grandson to ᐸᐦᐹᐢᑌᐤ pahpâstêw, **ᑳᐯᓵᑲᐢᑌᐠ reuben quinn** teaches ᓀᐦᐃᔭᐍᐏᐣ nêhîyawewin at University nuhelot'įne thaiyots'į nistameyimâkanak Blue Quills. He taught ᓀᐦᐃᔭᐍᐏᐣ nêhîyawewin at the Centre for Race and Culture in Edmonton for many years and at the University of Alberta. He was also a ceremony person and lodge keeper. He lives in amiskwaciy-wâskahikan (Edmonton).